KETO FOR CHRISTIANS

A BIBLICAL REFERENCE GUIDE TO EMBRACING THE KETO LIFESTYLE

BY BARBARA HALE

DISCLAIMER

The author of this book is not a trained medical professional and lays no claim to being an expert and does not provide medical advice. The publisher and author make no representations or warranties with respect to the accuracy or completeness of the contents of this work and specifically disclaim all warranties, including without limitation warranties of fitness for a particular purpose. All recipes/and or projects contained in this book have been tested for the authors own personal individual use/ and or consumption and are being provided to the reader as suggestions for their use. The author does not assume responsibility for any negative effects such as allergic reaction, rash, skin irritation or other occurrences. It is the reader's responsibility to read product labels and use at their own discretion.

This work is sold with the understanding that the publisher is not engaged in rendering medical, legal or other professional advice and strategies contained herein may not be suitable for every situation.

The information provided in this book is designed to provide helpful information on the subjects discussed. This book is not meant to be used, nor should it be used, to diagnose or treat any medical condition. For diagnosis or treatment of any medical problem, consult your own physician. The publisher and author are not responsible for any specific health or allergy needs that may require medical supervision and are not liable for any damages or negative health or allergy needs that may require medical supervision and are not liable for any damages or negative consequences from any person reading or following the information in this book. References are provided for informational purposes only and do not constitute endorsement of any websites or other sources. Readers should be aware that the websites listed in this book may change.

DEDICATION

With love and respect to my younger sister, Marylou Wood, without whom this book may never have been written. Your dedication and unending commitment to God and your spiritual growth are inspiring.

Your constant support, encouragement and loving spirit inspire me to reach for the stars.

I could not have accomplished this without you.

Thank you. I love you Mericat.

TABLE of Contents

So, whether you eat or drink, or whatever you do, do all to the glory of God.

I CORINTHIANS 10:~~30~~ 31

FORWARD

Romans 14:17

For the kingdom of God is not a matter of eating and drinking but of righteousness and peace and joy in the Holy Spirit.

As a student of the bible, I am often asked what the Bible tells us about being overweight. Good Christian people that have tried, and failed in their numerous attempts to shed pounds and lose weight are often frustrated with the diet books available on the market today. There are literally thousands of diet books being sold in stores and online. Everywhere you look, you can find diet books written by doctors, professionals, nutritionists, and laypeople telling you how to lose weight. Yet our nation is still in the midst of an obesity epidemic. Its not hard to know where the problem lies: these diet books were written to make money – they market to people's insecurities, fears, neurosis, and desperation! This book is not written for those reasons, but instead, to fill a need both spiritual and physical, for every Christian seeking to know God's will for their lives on developing and maintaining healthy heating habits. In short, to help Christians understand what the Bible says about obesity.

Over the past few years I've talked to people from all walks of life who have tried one diet or another. Some successfully, and others not so much. The one constant that held out during this time was that those on the Ketogenic Diet saw more consistent weight loss and enjoyed a dramatic change to their overall level of health. So much so, that I decided to try the Ketogenic Diet for myself and see how well I fared.

With God's encouragement through the study of His word I embarked on my own weight loss program following the Ketogenic Diet. Having lost some 50 plus pounds so far, I can honestly say that this is the most comprehensive and endurable diet I have ever tried. However, without seeking God's guidance along the way I doubt I could have sustained it or any diet, for any length of time. God is the key element in this entire process. Seeking His message for my journey was key to my daily success. Dedicated prayer and bible study to try and glean Gods instructions on healthy eating were the key elements to my success.

I encourage you to make Him an integral part of YOUR decision to start this or any weight loss program.

Proverbs 3: 5-6

"Trust in the Lord with all your heart, and do not lean on your own understanding. In all your ways acknowledge him, and he will make straight your paths."

INTRODUCTION

The main purpose of this book is to reach the millions of Christians that are struggling with obesity and health related issues due to overeating. As Christians, we have a vast source of help, strength, and encouragement to tap into that others do not. We often forget that. I'm writing here to remind us all that we have God's Word to help us on our path. We have our Bible.

Why consider the Bible when you want to go on a diet?

Just as with any other situation and circumstance in the Christian life, we need to seek God's enlightenment. We want to make sure we are doing God's will and growing in our walk with Him. The way to do that is through communication.

The Bible is the Christians Guide to Living. In order to communicate with God, you must dedicate yourself to Daily Bible Reading. Reading your Bible is your way to receive communication from God. In order to girder yourself and stay strong when attempting to change your eating habits you must be able to understand and put God's words into action. First, we pray, then we read the Bible to check for messages from God. It is the place He allowed His thoughts to be written down so Christians could learn to live a Spirit-filled life.

Because the Bible contains God's thoughts, recorded by men under the guidance of the Holy Spirit, it is different from any other book in the world. The Holy Spirit is at work any time a Christian reads the Bible, helping him or her to understand what is written. Reading your Bible at the same time you read your guide to creating healthier eating habits is a sure-fire way to win at both growing spiritually, and being successful in your weight loss endeavor!

By the grace of the Holy Spirit and righteous men willing to listen, God shows us who He is and what its like to know Him. His Word made plain for us to learn His plan for our lives. There is no greater source of wisdom, encouragement, understanding and direction for today's Christian.

The Bible carries one central, consistent message: God, who created us all in His image, desires a relationship with each and every one of us. A personal relationship. He calls us to know Him, and to put our trust in Him.

The Bible not only inspires us, it explains what God expects of us and how we are to live our lives. It may not answer all of the questions we might have, but enough of them. It shows us how to live with purpose and compassion. It teaches us how to relate to others. It also encourages us to rely on God for strength, direction, and to enjoy His love for us.

Knowing all of this, then it only stands to reason that we should rely on Him when we attempt to make changes in our life, and to walk the path towards better health.

"And those who know your name put their trust in you, for you, O Lord, have not forsaken those who seek you." Psalm 9:10

What better place to begin a new chapter in your life than by walking hand in hand beside our Lord and Savior?

"So, whether you eat or drink, or whatever you do, do all to the glory of God." I Corinthians 10:3̶8̶ 3)

If your reading this book then you are most likely a Christian looking for help to control your eating habits. As a Christian, it is safe to assume that you understand God's stand on sin, and that He expects you to make every effort to live as sinless a life a possible.

Modern day Christianity seems to have taken the stand that it can pick and choose which sins are acceptable, and which are not. Gluttony seems to be one of those sins that Christians like to ignore. We have no problem in labeling smoking and drinking as sins, idolatry and adultery, but for some reason obesity and

"DO YOU NOT KNOW THAT YOUR BODIES ARE TEMPLES OF THE HOLY SPIRIT, WHO IS IN YOU, WHOM YOU HAVE RECEIVED FROM GOD? YOU ARE NOT YOUR OWN; YOU WERE BOUGHT AT A PRICE. THEREFORE, HONOR GOD WITH YOUR BODIES." 1 CORINTHIANS 6:19-20

gluttony is accepted, or at the very least, tolerated.

Many Christians find it easy to dismiss the idea that overeating is a sin. However, God has told us that gluttony is most definitely a sin. If you need to, you can think of it as a form of idolatry – you are choosing to worship the feeling of comfort or pleasure that comes with overeating instead of taking heed of God's directions to treat our bodies as a Temple of God. 1 Corinthians 6:19-20 reminds us "Do you not know that your bodies are temples of the Holy Spirit, who is in you, whom you have received from God? You are not your own: you were bought at a price. Therefore, honor God with your bodies."

We are warned in Proverbs 23:20-21 "Do not join those who drink too much wine or gorge themselves on meat, for drunkards and gluttons become poor, and drowsiness clothes them in rags." Proverbs 28:7 declares, "He who keeps the law is a discerning son, but a companion of gluttons disgraces his father." Proverbs 23:2 proclaims, "Put a knife to your throat if you are given to gluttony."

This book is about losing weight. This book is for Christians. It is not just about losing weight, but doing so while growing spiritually and developing new, healthier habits that will honor God.

Let's begin to honor Him today and heed His call to control our appetites, rather than allowing them to control us.

"Therefore, I urge you, brothers and sisters, in view of God's mercy, to offer your bodies as a living sacrifice, holy and pleasing to God – this is your true and proper worship. Do not conform to the pattern of this world, but be transformed by the renewing of your mind. Then you will be able to test and approve what God's will is – His good, pleasing and perfect will." Romans 12: 1-2

THE SCIENCE BEHIND THE DIET

One of the toughest things to do when starting any diet is choosing which diet to start. There are literally hundreds of diets to choose from at any given time. A few examples are The Dash Diet, which was designed to help people lower their high blood pressure; the Mediterranean Diet which was developed to reflect food patterns typical of Crete, Greece and southern Italy; the Flexitarian Diet was developed to help people reap the benefits of a vegetarian diet while still enjoying animal products in moderation; and of course, Americas most famous, Weight Watchers diet. Each of these diets promise all kinds of things- effortless weight loss without sacrifice, without hunger. You'll get to eat cookies, your skin will clear up, your wrinkles will go away, and dogs and small children will love you. They share their gimmicks, tricks, and hooks to get you excited enough to begin, but fall short of explaining the science behind their promises. Usually because there is no science. Just fad after fad that someone has thought up to make money. You know how their story ends. You start, you fall, you fail. And you end up right back where you started, very often, having added a couple of extra pounds to top it all off.

This book is different: because this diet is different. First of all, you won't be doing this alone. You will have the greatest support system in the universe – God. Strengthening your walk with the Lord, learning to control your appetites as directed in the Bible, and taking responsibility for the human temple God has given you will strengthen your will and light your path.

The keto diet is much more than a fad diet; it will actually teach you a new way of eating that is not just for the time being, but forever. It is sustainable. You will be training your body to treat food in a whole new way.

The keto diet was originally developed by researchers and doctors for children with epilepsy. Studies proved that this special high-fat, very low-cab and protein plan helped to control, if not eliminate, seizures in children and adults with this disease. Similar to the Atkins diet, Adults with epilepsy often eat modified Atkins diets to help control seizures. Atkins is a similar eating plan which drastically restricts carbs, and promotes more fats and protein. The differences between the two diets are worth researching on your part so you get a better understanding of how each one works.

Let's take a moment and reflect on what we are actually talking about here. The word "diet" has such a negative connotation in today's world. It brings to mind images of celery sticks and carrots, starvation, and a never-ending struggle with will power. It implies that someone has issues with eating habits, most specifically, overeating. But that's not what the word should mean to us. If you check a dictionary, you'll find that the word diet is simply a reference to the type of foods that a person, community, or animal habitually eats. I can also mean a "special course of food to which one restricts oneself, either to lose weight, or for medical reasons." And there's that word no one likes…restrict.

In this book we are going to use the definition that makes us feel and think positively about the path we are about to embark on – it's not going to bring to mind those negative images, and we are going to think of the word "restrict" in a positive way when we discuss the changes we are going to make. God wants us to be healthy, He instructs us to be diligent in taking care of the body that he has given us, the temple he has provided. So, in following His lead, we are going to begin to think about the keto diet as merely a habitual way of eating to create a healthy body. We aren't going to "restrict" our foods, we may eliminate some, and we may contain portions on others, but we will not think of our new-way-of-eating as depriving ourselves – but instead, embrace God's desire for us to have healthy, happy bodies and consider this new-way-of-eating as the right path to lead us towards that goal.

BENEFITS OF THE KETO DIET

Burning fat for fuel establishes a more consistent energy level and doesn't spike your blood glucose, so you won't experience the highs and lows you do when eating large amounts of carbohydrates. Having more energy comes with its own benefits – you can get more done and feel less tired while doing so! Other research suggests that the ketogenic diet can provide additional benefits such as:

- Improved brain function
- Reduced blood pressure
- Improve levels of HDL (good) and LDL (bad) cholesterol
- Reduce triglyceride levels
- Reduce blood sugar and insulin resistance (type 2 diabetes)
- Results in weight loss

WHATEXACTLY IS KETOSIS?

ke·to·sis
noun: ketosis

a metabolic state characterized by raised levels of ketone bodies in the body tissues, which is typically pathological in conditions such as diabetes, or may be the consequence of a diet that is very low in carbohydrates.

What causes ketosis? Your body normally utilizes carbohydrates as its main energy source. When it doesn't have enough carbs from food for your body to burn for energy, it burns fat instead. Fatty acid production in fat tissue is stimulated by epinephrine and glucagon, and is inhibited by insulin. Insulin is one of the hormones the pancreas secretes in the presence of carbohydrates. Insulin's purpose is to keep blood glucose levels in check by acting like a driver, pushing the glucose into cells. If insulin was not secreted, blood glucose levels would get out of control. Ketosis is a normal metabolic process your body does to keep it running smoothly. When your body utilizes fat for fuel it produces "ketones". Most cells in your body use ketones and

What exactly is Ketosis? The metabolic state of ketosis simply means that the quantity of ketone bodies in the blood have reached higher-than-normal levels. When the body is in a ketogenic state, this means that lipid energy metabolism is intact. The body will start breaking down your own body fat to fuel the body's normal, everyday functions.

glucose for fuel. The main goal of the keto diet is to keep you in nutritional ketosis all the time. For those of you just starting the keto diet, it may take your body anywhere from four to eight weeks to become fully "keto-adapted."

FATS (FATTY ACIDS) AND PROTEIN   ARE ESSENTIAL FOR SURVIVAL. THERE IS NO SUCH THING AS AN ESSENTIAL CARBOHYDRATE.

Once you become keto-adapted, glycogen (the glucose stored in your muscles and liver) decreases, you will carry less water weight, your muscle endurance increases, and your overall energy levels are higher than ever. One additional perk, is that if you kick yourself out of ketosis by eating too many carbs, you will return to the state of ketosis much sooner that when you were not keto-adapted.

After three to four days of restricting your carbs to less than 20 - 25 grams per day, your body will go into "ketosis" and begin burning protein and fat as fuel. Your body will begin to break down its stored fat and convert it to glucose. Studies consistently show that a keto diet helps people lose more weight and improve energy levels throughout the day. Being in ketosis and eating more fats and proteins will diminish your hunger and make you feel full longer. The improved energy levels and increased satiety are attributed to most of the calories coming from fat, which is calorically dense and very slow to digest.

I must add here, that if you have diabetes, a low-carb diet can greatly improve or even begin to reverse the condition. But as with any diet, you should always consult your doctor before beginning a low-carb diet.

All forms of dietary carbohydrates are made up of sugar (glucose). I think it would be helpful to show you a partial list of exactly what "carbohydrates" are in regard to our average American diet. These are what are commonly known as "hidden sugars." You'll find hidden sugars in most commonly packaged foods such as breads, bagels, pastas, and cereals. To avoid overeating on high-calorie foods, or pre-packaged foods with these hidden-sugars, try to fill up on green, leafy vegetables that will provide nutrient laden sources of fuel instead. Your highest priority should be high-nutrient, low-carb eating at this point.

It is imperative that you learn to read labels on everything you purchase for consumption. Food in our grocery stores are full of hidden sugars and other unhealthy man-made preservatives that we simply do not want to put into our bodies.

As a side note, let me say that it is crucial to drink plenty of water when beginning the keto diet. Trips to the bathroom will increase but this is absolutely normal. Processed foods contain large quantities of sodium, once you begin to cut out the processed foods and begin eating more whole, natural foods instead the sudden change in diet causes a sudden drop in sodium intake. This drop in sodium helps to "flush" out the excess water being stored in your body, so more frequent urination naturally occurs. A reduction in carbohydrates also reduces insulin levels, which in turn causes your kidneys to release excess stored sodium. Between the reduced intake of sodium, and the flushing of excess sodium, your body begins to eliminate much more water than usual, and you end up low on sodium and other electrolytes. This loss of essential electrolytes is what causes the ill feeling associated with the "Keto Flu."

Many may wonder if God thinks this is good for us, why does He allow us to get sick in the process? That is an age-old question that can only be partial answered here. If you're not overweight due a medical condition, then overindulging and eating the wrong foods is what placed you in your current situation. There is no looking past that at this point. Your body is in the shape that it is due to thoughtlessness, neglect, or being uneducated in good nutrition. I'm not saying this to make you feel bad or guilty, I'm not deliberately being mean or vicious, I'm just stating facts. We are all human, and we all make mistakes. And I honestly believe that being overweight is a mistake; untll you understand that gluttony is a sin as stated in the bible. Once you fully understand this, it's your choice whether or not to follow the Lord and work on your eating habits to heal your body. It is going to take some work to get it back to what God intended it to be. The simple fact is, any change in your routine diet can be an extreme change for your body to adjust to. It's a shock to the system that has been fueling itself in the same way for years. It will take some time to adjust to this new-way-of-eating.

The bible tells us in Romans 5: 3-4 "More than that, we rejoice in our sufferings, knowing that suffering produces endurance, and endurance produces character, and character produces hope."

Knowing and understanding that this process will not only heal our bodies, but that it will change our character and our soul as well should give us hope. While we are training our bodies a new way to fuel itself, we should be increasing our prayer time, our bible reading time, and our communication with God will improve as well. Sometimes a little suffering is good for the soul.

During the first few weeks of your transition into ketosis, the body has to go through a metabolic shift. You will likely experience some degree of fatigue and brain fog. You may experience some dehydration because of the ketonic-induced diuresis and water loss from depletion of glycogen stores. You may experience headaches, nausea, and sleepiness. It's called the Keto-Flu for a reason – you feel miserable just as if you had the regular flu! The up side is that for most people, it only lasts for a few days. In rare cases it's been known to last from a day to a week, or longer. Everyone's bodies are different, and some people handle the switch over better than others. You may consider starting your new WOE (way of eating) on the weekend or sometime when you're able to get a good deal of rest to deal with the symptoms. Once the body gets used to manufacturing ketones as its main energy source, the body actually has more energy than it previously had. Bonus: you won't have to be fighting through all those low-blood-sugar crashes your high carb meals previously gave you.

Prayers for Strength will be helpful during this time.

Lord, I'm afraid of what the future holds. I don't know if I can face the challenges ahead of me today. My body is weak and I'm feeling sick. Lend me your strength so I can walk like Jesus through the uncertainty.

Amen.

You may feel like giving up, or that this diet just isn't for you. Stay strong, fight those urges, pray for help, and push through this phase! Suffering for a week to lose years of weight gain and enjoy even more years of good health will be worth the effort. I promise.

Trust in the LORD with all your heart and lean not on your own understanding; in all your ways submit to him, and he will make your paths straight.

Proverbs 3:5-6

This isn't to say that suffering is mandatory, and that in order for spiritual growth to occur, you must suffer. The good news is, it is possible to lessen the symptoms of the keto flu. First, you have to understand why your body is reacting this way.

Your body has been burning glucose for energy all of your life, so it's FULL of enzymes that are waiting to deal with the carbs you eat (and just waiting to store them as fat). But with the depletion of carbohydrates, your body now needs to make adjustments to the type of enzymes it produces. It needs to begin manufacturing enzymes that burn fat for fuel instead of carbs. The transition period between these two totally different ways of creating and utilizing the body's enzymes results in what is known as the keto-flu.

Have faith. God's desire is not for you to suffer, but for your body to heal itself.

> For I know the plans I have for you, declares the Lord, plans for welfare and not for evil, to give you a future and a hope.
>
> Jerimiah 29:11

Let's review what we have read so far regarding the keto-flu; the keto-flu is the result of three significant factors:

1. adaptation to keto,
2. electrolyte imbalance and
3. withdrawal from carbohydrates.

In order to lessen the symptoms, or to avoid them altogether, be sure to avoid dehydration. Drink plenty of water (yes, coffee and tea do count here), and watch your electrolytes. Reducing your carb intake results in the body getting rid of excess insulin which means you'll lose lots of fluids that your body has been retaining. This causes the rapid weight loss most people see in their first few days of ketosis, it's mostly water. Along with that water, the bodies electrolytes like sodium, magnesium and potassium are also flushed. It's important to replace those electrolytes in order for your body to function at its best.

Adding salt to your meals, eating more fat and drinking bullion will help. Butter everything, bacon everything, eat fatty meats and put heavy cream in your coffee. The fat consumption will force your body to speed up the transition. It may seem counterintuitive, but it will work.

Another thing to watch is your protein intake. Many people make the mistake of overeating protein because think of this along the lines of the Atkins diet – but the boy can transform protein into glucose. So, if you eat too much of it in the first days it will slow down the transition. Go for fatty meat and cheese if you can, add fat to protein shakes etc.

Eat foods that are generally saltier like pickles and bacon. To replace other electrolytes, try to eat more of the foods listed below.

- For potassium: eat avocados, nuts, dark leafy greens such as spinach and kale, salmon, plain yogurt, and mushrooms.
- To replace magnesium: eat nuts, dark chocolate, artichokes, spinach and fish.
- Calcium can be added by eating cheese, leafy greens, broccoli, seafood, and almonds.
- Replace Phosphorus by eating meats, cheeses, nuts, seeds, and dark chocolate.
- Chloride can be replaced by eating most vegetables, olives,

Keep in mind that the symptoms of the keto-flu will fade over the next few days, and you'll come out on the other side a stronger, more alert, and lighter individual!

He gives power to the faint, and to him who has no might he increases strength. Even youths shall faint and be weary, and young men shall fall exhausted; but they who wait for the Lord shall renew their strength; they shall mount up with wings like eagles; they shall run and not be weary; they shall walk and not faint.

Isiah 40: 29-31

God promises to be faithful if we choose to follow him and strive for a true relationship. Learning a healthier way of eating to sustain your body and soul is proof positive that you yearn for a stronger walk with Christ. Proclaim your faith, walk the talk, and most of all, believe. Believe that you can have a stronger, healthier body that will be worthy to be called a Temple of the Holy Spirit.

PREPARING THE MIND AND SOUL

I urge you to seek the guidance of the Lord before you begin this, or any other journey that will completely change your way of life. Praying, bible reading, and even fasting can help create a strong communication pathway that will give you the strength of will and commitment necessary to begin your weight loss journey.

Because the Bible contains God's thoughts, recorded by men under the influence and guidance of the Holy Spirit, the Holy Spirit is at work anytime a Christian reads the Bible, helping him or her to understand what is written. The Holy Spirit is present whenever you read the Bible, beside you, guiding you, helping you to understand the message God has waiting for you.

PRAYER LEADS THE WAY

"All Scripture is God-breathed and is useful for teaching, rebuking, correcting and, training in righteousness, so that the man of God may be thoroughly equipped for every good work,"

2 Timothy 3:16-17

The Bible is full of answers about how we are to live. Hebrews 4:12 tells us "For the word of God is living and active. Sharper than any double-edged sword, it penetrates even to dividing soul and spirit, joints and marrow; it judges the thoughts and attitudes of the heart."

Reading the Bible can judge and correct your attitudes, and can give you great hope and encouragement as you begin this new way of eating. Don't believe for one second that this is an easy change; you've been surviving on man-made, artificial food products for years that have caused havoc and chaos within your organs, and your mind. It can be done, and you will be successful. But as God has forewarned us, Satan will always be there to put obstacles in our way.

Get yourself spiritually ready, and take on the full armor of God. Prepare yourself to wage a war on your emotions, old habits, and desires of the flesh, and most importantly, Satan.

"Therefore, put on the full armor of God, so that when the day of evil comes, you may be able to withstand, and after you have done everything, to stand firm. Stand therefore, with the belt of truth buckled around your waist, with the breastplate of righteousness in place, and with your feet fitted with the readiness that comes from the gospel of peace. In addition to all this, take up the shield of faith, with which you can extinguish all the flaming arrows of the evil one. Take the helmet of salvation and the sword of the Spirit, which is the word of God."

Ephesians 6:13-17

The Keto way of eating has gained momentum as a science-based solution for weight control. More people than ever are embracing this very low-carb, high-fat diet for months, and even years. Many have created a lifestyle of it. They find they are healthier, leaner and become more mentally focused than ever before. All of this happens once you successfully recondition your mind and soul, and your body transitions from using carbohydrate to using fat and ketones as your body's natural fuel source.

In order to be successful with the keto diet, we need to understand that Satan attacks us in unique and mysterious ways. Ephesians 6:12 tells us that the conflict with Satan is spiritual, and as a result no tangible weapons can be effectively employed against him and his minions. We can imagine the things that Satan will use to tempt us: modern day food delicacies as well as the American staples of every day eating, all packed full of hidden sugars and preservatives that destroy the good health we are striving for. Common things like pizza, cakes, candies, pastas and all forms of carbohydrate saturated foods are just a few of the weapons Satan will use against us!

He will attempt to inflict self-doubt and feelings of unworthiness. However, the Bible is very clear that when we follow all the instructions faithfully, we will be able to stand strong, and be victorious. Have faith in God, and have faith in YOURSELF. Developing an attitude of self-respect, self-love, and practicing forgiveness for yourself when you slip is paramount to your success in this diet, as well as your life in general. Learn, then practice to love yourself as God has loved you.

You are altogether beautiful, my love; there is no flaw in you.
Song of Solomon 4:7

Putting on the "full amour" of God is a daily task. Much like getting bathed and dressed for the day, reading the Bible and getting our attitudes and goals straight are what will bring us success as we work on developing new, healthier eating habits and breaking old thought processes.

Be constantly vigilant and aware that Satan is the "father of lies" as described in John 8:44. He will work to weaken our resolve by whispering small lies such as "one bite won't hurt" or "just a taste is fine." He will bombard our senses with sights, smells and memories of a previous way of eating that will test our resolve daily. He can get us to "lie" to ourselves by suggesting that we just can't do it; that we don't have the strength, will power, or resolve to make this work. Deception is high on the list of things God considers to be an abomination. A "lying tongue" is one of the things He describes as "detestable to Him" (Proverbs 6:16 -17). Because of this, God teaches us to put on the TRUTH of our own sanctification and deliverance, to praise God and voice our strengths instead of falling victim to Satan's destructive lies. Take the time to read the passages over and over, to get the full impact of what God is telling us to do. Pray and praise God for our faith, of which Christ is "the author and perfecter" (Hebrews 12:2) – for your faith is like a golden shield, precious, solid, and substantial that will sustain you as you work on finding your path to a new eating lifestyle.

To love God, is to love his creations. YOU are one of His most magnificent designs. You are worthy of love, worthy of forgiveness, and worthy to be called a Child of God. Satan has no power over you, unless you consent.

For you formed my inward parts; you knitted me together in my mother's womb. I praise you, for I am fearfully and wonderfully made. Wonderful are your works; my soul knows it very well. My frame was not hidden from you, when I was being made in secret, intricately woven in the depths of the earth.

Psalms 139: 13-15

PLANNING PHASE

Commit your work to the Lord, and your plans will be established.
Proverbs 16:3

For every successful dieter, you'll find another who had a dismal experience and gave up after just a few days. This is most likely because they left God out of the equation. It's an unfortunate loss that can be avoided if we just follow God's instructions and take the time to lay out a solid plan.

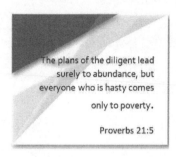

The plans of the diligent lead surely to abundance, but everyone who is hasty comes only to poverty.

Proverbs 21:5

The keto diet is based on ratios, much like the USDA'S FOOD PYRAMID. The keto pyramid is based on the body's macronutrient needs in a fat-burning environment. The second most important thing you need to do before you start shopping and cooking your way to a new healthier life, is to figure out how many calories you need and then use that to figure out your macros per day. Macros is the shortened term for macronutrients. It's important to get the right balance of macros so your body has the correct amounts of each element to create the fat-burning environment essential to your weight loss goals.

Macronutrients are the elements that foods are made up of. They are fat, protein and carbohydrates. Each type of macro provides a specific number of calories (or energy) per gram consumed. It breaks down like this:

- Fat provides approximately 9 calories per gram
- Protein provides approximately 4 calories per gram
- Carbohydrates provide approximately 4 calories per gram.

The number of calories you consume daily should be tailored to your body, activity levels, and goals. The number of calories you should eat depends on a few factors, including:

- Current lean body weight (total body weight minus body fat)
- Daily activity levels (do you work in an office, wait tables, are you a stay at home mom)
- Workout regime? If so:
  - The types of workouts (weight lifting, cardio, or both)
  - Hours per week of each type
- What your Goals are:
  - Lose weight
  - Maintain weight
  - Gain muscle

Following the example of the USDAs pyramid, a sample 2000 calorie a day plan on the Keto Pyramid breaks down like this:

- Fat = 65 – 75%
- Protein = 20 -25%
- Carbohydrates = 5%

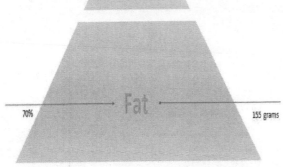

2000-Calorie Daily Ketogenic Diet

% OF DAILY CALORIES — Carbs — IN GRAMS
5% — 25 grams

Protein — 20% — 125 grams

Fat — 70% — 155 grams

65 to 70% of calories should come from fat, 20-25% of calories consumed should come from protein, and the remaining 5% or so from carbohydrates. So, again, it looks like this:

- Fat = 65-75%
- Protein=20-25%
- Carbohydrates= 5%

This may vary a little depending on your individual needs, but it's a good place to start. Now you just need to figure out how these percentages fit into your diet. There are numerous ketogenic-based macro calculators available online, such as tasteaholics.com/ keto-calculator and ketogains.com/ketogains-calculator. You can use a site like freedieting.com to plug in your calories and macronutrient percentages or any one of the numerous apps available. I personally use My Fitness Pal app and log each meal into my iPhone. If you subscribe to social media platforms, you can definitely find keto-friendly support groups on Face Book that can help you figure this out if you need.

On the keto diet you're not meant to be depriving your body, you're meant to be feeding it ideal nutrition that makes it work more efficiently. Simply by eliminating sugars, cutting out carbs and eating keto foods, most people will eat fewer calories than usual and start losing weight pretty consistently. Which is great – but following the diet this way can increase your likelihood of hitting a weight loss plateau and not knowing what to do next.

When you start tracking, you'll quickly understand how many carbs you've actually been eating, and it may come as quite a shock. There are plenty of tracking apps available as well. The ones which are most popular are the ones that usually have the best food databases, which is an essential part of the program. When choosing a tracking app, make sure that you choose one that tracks your macros and allows you to set macro goals for the day. Ideally, you should also track your sodium, potassium and magnesium intake to make sure that your electrolytes are in balance. Ultimately, the best tracking app is the app that you actually use. Again, do a google search for keto macro tracking apps an you'll come up with dozens of them. Choose the one that fits your needs most accurately.

Getting your macros correct is the most important aspect of starting down the path of a ketogenic diet. You may think you've got what it takes to make the switch to keto without tracking your macronutrients, but you're probably wrong. No matter what your diet has been to this point, keto will be a big change. If you're coming from a standard American diet (SAD) background, your carbs will go way down, protein may either go up or down, and fat will go way up. This keto diet most likely goes against everything you've done before. So, tracking your macro's gives you feedback and allows you to troubleshoot until you get the hang of it. Keto will be a big change. Embrace it wholeheartedly and your success will be inevitable!

God filled our world with healthy, nutritious foods for us to delight in. Yet, today's society has accepted a way of eating that includes foods processed with sugars and preservatives that poison our bodies over the long term. Through no fault of our own, we grew up embracing the eating habits of our American culture. Getting back to basics, letting go of the need and desire to gorge instead of just using food for fuel, is one of our main goals. You'll have to have an eating plan in place to meet these particular goals. In order to get your plan ready, you'll need to start by getting your house in shape.

This means you'll need to go through your refrigerator and cabinets, all those goodie-hiding places you have around (yes, I know you probably hide ding-dongs or candy to keep on hand for sweet-attacks or so your kids can't find them) and clean house! You need to get rid of everything that has a significant carb count. Everything goes. Or so it may seem... No fair keeping just one piece of candy "just in case." It all has to go. It will probably hurt a little; these bags of popcorn and chocolates; Little Debbie cakes and donuts have been your friends for many years. Now it's time to see the truth and understand, they were never really your friends. The comfort you derived from eating them was a false sense of well-being that lasted only as long as you were chewing. They were instead, enemies of the worst kind. They were, and continue to be, saboteurs and Satan's weapons to keep you overweight, unhappy, unhealthy, and out of God's grace! For if we choose these foods over seeking God's true plan for us, then we have fallen victim to Satan's plan to destroy us. He will destroy our bodies, deconstructing the Temple of the Holy Spirit, until we can no longer hear the voice of God. He will push the joy of the Lord out of our hearts and souls, slowly replacing it with doubt, despair and the destructive feelings of worthlessness and self-loathing. Planning a different path is essential!

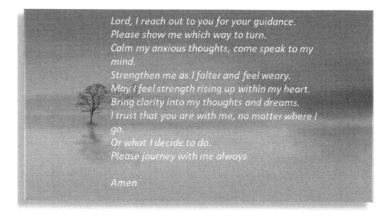

Lord, I reach out to you for your guidance.
Please show me which way to turn.
Calm my anxious thoughts, come speak to my mind.
Strengthen me as I falter and feel weary.
May I feel strength rising up within my heart.
Bring clarity into my thoughts and dreams.
I trust that you are with me, no matter where I go.
Or what I decide to do.
Please journey with me always

Amen

(Prayer for endurance, and wisdom in the face of fear and doubt)

BEGINNING THE JOURNEY TO YOUR NEW LIFESTYLE

Rid your home of harmful foods

I know this will be hard for many of you. Getting rid of perfectly good foods is just not a "normal" thing to do. Although at this point, we all understand that what we are getting rid of can't actually be considered "perfectly good" food. It still stands to reason, that somewhere, someone can benefit from what we do not want. Check to see If your church has a food bank, or offers food boxes to the needy. If not, try your local community center. If all else fails, ask about having a church wide garage sale and hand out food boxes yourself! Help others while helping yourself. Having tempting, unhealthy foods laying around is a sure- fire way to meet failure head on. Its best to reduce and remove anything that can trigger an impulse binge or create unnecessary cravings that will only make things harder for yourself.

Acts 20:35

In all things I have shown you that by working hard in this way we must help the weak and remember the words of the Lord Jesus, how he himself said, 'It is more blessed to give than to receive.'

Most of us do not live in our homes alone, so it's best to sit down and discuss your dieting plans with your loved ones. Not only will you need their support while your transforming your body and soul, but you don't want to throw something out that may mean a great deal to someone else in the house! You can arrange to keep their non-keto friendly food stuffs in a separate area where out-of-sight is out-of-mind to prevent struggle and defeat. You will need your family's support, so be thoughtful and respectful of their needs and desires as you begin your new way of eating, and you will find them encouraging and helpful along your journey. Remember, God does not always speak to people at the same time, and although you feel God's plan for you is clear, it may not be to your family members. Use love and diplomacy in your discussions with them and you may even find them willing participants and part of a newly created support group! It always works best if a family follows the same eating habits, but it isn't necessary.

Start your clean out by getting rid of the following items:

• SUGARED FOODS AND DRINKS

All the refined packaged sugars, soda, fruit juices, desserts, pastries, candy bars, milk, etc. Things like crackers have

• LEGUMES

Get rid of all beans, peas and lentils. They are extremely dense with carbohydrates. A one cup serving of beans alone contains more than three times the amount of carbs you want to consume in a day.

• FRUITS

Most fruits also tend to be fairly rich in carbohydrates, primarily the simple sugars, glucose and fructose. Instead of spending the entire carb budget on 1 or 2 pieces of fruit, it would be better spent eating plenty of low-carb vegetables, which are much more nutritious, calorie for calorie.

- STARCHES AND GRAINS

Your bread, croissants, rolls, bagels, cereal, pasta, rice and potatoes have to go. Along with those goes your flour, quinoa, oats and corn.

- PROCESSED POLYUNSATURATED FATS AND OILS.

You'll need to eliminate trans fats like shortening and margarine, anything that says hydrogenated or partially hydrogenated. Get rid of all vegetable oils and most seed oils including sunflower, safflower, canola, soybean, grapeseed, and corn oil.

***Olive oil, extra-virgin olive oil, avocado oil, and coconut oil are the keto-friendly oils you want on hand

When you see how bare your pantry seems after you finish the clean-out, consider that most of those things you had hiding in there were meant for "long term" storage and are usually high in carbs and chock full of unhealthy additives and preservatives. Just as you don't need them in your pantry, you definitely don't need them inside your body!

And God said, "Behold, I have given you every plant yielding seed that is on the face of all the earth, and every tree with seed in its fruit. You shall have them for food."

Genesis 1:29

SHOPPING

The next step is to restock your pantry, fridge and freezer. It's time to go shopping for delicious, keto-friendly foods that will help you lose weight, become healthier, and feel and look great

As in all things, its best to start off simple. Stock up on the basics and you'll always be ready to prepare healthy, keto-friendly meals and snacks.

THE BASICS

Be sure to pick up these basics first thing.

Remember that God calls us to be wise stewards of our money. You don't have to rush out and buy everything listed on the pages here, but instead, put some thought into it and get those things you know you'll use first. Read Luke 16:1-13 to get more insight.

- Water, coffee, and tea
- All spices and herbs (check the labels for added sugars!)
- Sweeteners, including Stevia and erythritol
- Lemon and lime juice
- Low-carb condiments such as mayonnaise, mustard, pesto, and sriracha
- Broths (chicken, beef, bone)
- Pickled and fermented foods like pickles, kimchi, and sauerkraut

- Nuts and seeds: including macadamia nuts, pecans, almonds, walnuts, hazelnuts, pine nuts, flaxseed, chia seeds, and pumpkin seeds.

Once you've gotten the basics, it time to concentrate on those items that will make up the majority of your menus.

MEATS

Any type of meat is actable for the keto diet. Enjoy chicken, beef, lamb, pork, turkey, etc. A lot of people will tell you to purchase grass-fed/organic meats if they are available, but this isn't necessary and it can impact your budget. Just be sure to get as fresh as possible and you'll be fine. One of the perks about the keto diet is that it is more than acceptable to eat the fat and skin on the chicken. Fish and seafood have a prominent place in the keto diet! Eggs also hold an important place here.

VEGATABLES

Avoid all types of potatoes, yams, corn, and legumes like beans, lentils, and peas. You can eat all non-starchy veggies including broccoli, asparagus, mushrooms, cucumbers, lettuce, onions, peppers, brussels sprouts, zucchini, eggplant, olives, zucchini, yellow squash and cauliflower.

FRUITS

Most fruits are off limits on the keto diet due to the high levels of sugars they contain. A Single banana for example, has around 25 grams of carbohydrates! However, you may eat small amounts of berries every day such as strawberries, raspberries, blackberries, and blueberries. Lemon and lime juices are great for adding flavor to your meals. Avocados are also low in carbs and full of healthy fat.

DAIRY

Always eat full-fat dairy like butter, sour cream, heavy whipping cream, cheese, cream cheese, and unsweetened yogurt. Avoid milk and skim milk, as well as sweetened yogurts as they contain great amounts of sugar. Although technically not dairy, you can enjoy unsweetened almond and coconut milks as well.

FATS AND OILS

Avocado oil, olive oil, butter, lard, and bacon fat are great for cooking as well as general consumption. Avocado oil has a high smoke point (it does not burn or smoke until it reaches 550 F), which is ideal for searing meats and frying in a wok.

Add beef and chicken bouillon to the list as well. Make sure the bouillon cubes have at least 1 gram of sodium. Why? When carbs are cut, we rapidly deplete our store of glycogen (what carbohydrates are converted into when we eat them). For every gram of glycogen we lose, we lose 3 grams of water. Adding the bouillon will help prevent dehydration and improve the way you feel on the diet. Water isn't enough on keto: you need enough sodium as well. Drinking chicken broth is absolutely critical to combat the keto flu.

YOUR KITCHEN

There are certain items that could make your life much simpler in the kitchen, but these are definitely not must-haves. If you feel that they would benefit your diet plan, and you have the money to spare, then following is a list of kitchen items that would be useful.

FOOD SCALE

A must have for anyone serious about weight loss. A food scale comes in quite handy for measuring your foods to make sure you are counting your macros and portions correctly. You can measure solids, or liquid food stuffs and be sure to get the perfect amount every time. It's not as easy to "guesstimate", but it can be done. A food scale used in conjunction with a carb counting app will help to ensure you hit your weight loss goals more quickly.

FOOD PROCESSOR

A food processor has more power than a typical blender when it's time to blend foods together for making sauces, or simply chopping down tough vegetables like cauliflower and broccoli. The food processor can also be used for kneading, making batters, slicing, chopping, cutting, shredding, grinding, or mincing. They can perform the task at hand with high efficiency in no time at all.

SPIRALIZER

Spiralizers make vegetables into noodles or ribbons within seconds. Vegetables like zucchini are naturally gluten-free, light in calories, carbs, and sugars which make them a great substitute for flour-based pastas. By spiralizing, you're naturally eating more vegetables without even noticing! Eating a bowl full of spiralized veggies will fool your taste buds into believing that you're enjoying your favorite pasta dishes while your waistline realizes the benefits of a healthy eating habit.

ELECTRIC HAND MIXER

Perhaps the best advantage of an electric hand mixer is the cost. Much less expensive than a stand mixer, the hand mixer also takes up less space in the kitchen. It's perfect for small jobs like blending or mixing cream cheese dishes, beating egg whites and whipping cream. If you've ever had to mix egg whites by hand, your arm muscles will thank you for investing in an electric hand mixer!

CAST IRON PANS

If you own cast iron pots and pans, now's the time to get them out. Cooking in cast iron is much healthier than using Teflon coated or other chemical treated pans, and they last pretty much forever. However, if you don't presently own these, do not by any means feel like you must go out and buy them! Whatever you currently have in the way of pots and pans is perfectly acceptable. Remember, the goal is to learn to cook and eat healthy, not to break the bank!

PLAN YOUR MEALS

Once you've changed your diet to eliminate processed and sugar-laden foods, you'll need to plan your meals each day to contain only keto-friendly, healthy foods. You can plan your meals every day or a week in advance. Some people plan out a month in advance to alleviate the possibility of cheating or finding themselves in tempting situations. Planning your meals provides you the opportunity to know exactly what to shop for, and keeps you from spending excess money on items you don't necessarily need at the moment. Another benefit of meal planning is the cost savings. Following a keto diet doesn't necessarily have to be expensive, but it certainly can become expensive if you are regularly running to the store for items you forgot, getting takeout, or letting food go to waste in the fridge Planning your meals ensures your success and enables you to remain on your diet for longer periods of time without interruption.

Because the ketogenic diet follows a specific breakdown of your calories it can be difficult to follow without proper planning. By doing all that planning for the whole week in one go, you reduce the stress of figuring out what to eat each day. You also save a lot of time, because you are not starting from scratch each day.

By creating a meal plan, you only need to go to the store once, and you know you won't be buying anything that will go to waste. So, how does it work? For me, I found it easier to split up my meal planning, shopping, and meal prep so I wasn't trying to do to much all at once and get overwhelmed. Since I prefer to do my shopping on Saturday afternoons to avoid the early morning crowds at my local Wal-Mart, so I decided to do my actual meal planning on Saturday mornings. The kids play nicely on their own for a couple of hours, freeing me up to sit down and think.

Choose a time that is as distraction-free as possible and give yourself a good hour – especially when first starting out. Once you get the hang of it, meal planning should only take you about 20 – 30 minutes.

Remember, meal planning is not a "one-size-fits-all" absolute – it's all about figuring out what works for you and developing your own system.

I won't go into exact steps here, you've all most likely done meal planning for the week before. This is the same thing. Start with looking at your average "standard" week schedule. Do you have time for a sit-down breakfast, or do you wake up and fly out the door? Does your workplace have a microwave where you can warm up your lunch? Do you tend to need a snack in the afternoons? If you're a stay at home mom like me, do you eat a snack with the kids when they get home from school? Having those snacks planned will go a long way in curbing your spur-of-the-moment eating binges!

If you do Taco Tuesdays and have pizza every Friday night, fear not—there are great keto tacos, and keto pizza recipes to keep the traditions going with a minimum of chaos that comes with change.

There will be those times when you spend all day running around and don't have time to cook. That's when having some prepared cook-ahead-foods will come in handy. Breakfast muffins, mini egg casseroles and others are great to have on hand in the refrigerator. Be sure to plan ahead and bake some of these handy grab-n-go meals and keep them in the fridge for those days when nothing seems to go right!

When you write down a meal plan for a week you can count how many meals you need to make. For example, do you need 6 breakfasts, 4 lunches, 2 dinners and 2 grab-n-go dinners? Be sure to write it all down and then keep it handy on the pantry door or fridge. Keep a list of what items you'll need for each day.

When you first get started, I recommend using your favorite keto recipes and each week add a new recipe to try each week. Keep it simple, you don't want to over whelm yourself from the start. One new recipe a week is enough to add a little variety without causing you too much stress.

Keep a cooler of on-the-go snacks available on those days when you know you'll be running around, it will come in handy. And for dinner, put a slow-cooker meal on first thing in the morning so that at the end of the day you'll have something ready. Another great idea is to use left-overs on those evenings after a long, busy day.

Once you have your meals planned and your recipes selected, it's time to make your shopping list. Use some common sense at this point, and check to see what you already have on hand in the pantry and refrigerator. You don't want to waste any money buying items you already have. When you have accomplished that, it's time to write your shopping list.

And there you have it – a few simple steps to get you started meal planning. Remember, practice makes perfect. Don't worry if it takes you a really long time to do this the first few times; it will get faster and easier with practice.

KEEP IT SIMPLE

Don't stress, don't worry, be happy. Remember who you have walking along side of you, and when you begin to grow anxious – stop. Breath. Ask for help. Ask for peace. Keep it simple. It's just food, it's just eating.

> *We are not called to be like other Christians, we are called to be like Christ.*

One of the top secrets to the keto-diet success is to repeat certain favorite meals each day or week. This can minimize your time planning meals, and avoid cooking fatigue. Try eating the same breakfast every day so you don't even have to think about it, you just get up and know what to eat. You can also cook larger quantities of dinner foods and save the leftovers for lunch the next day. You don't have to spend your time cooking up extravagant meals. Keeping it simple and making it work for your particular lifestyle is the key.

Choose fresh food over fast food. Discover your own favorite, soothing beverage to help take the edge off. I prefer a hot mug of Chi Tea at the end of a busy day. It relaxes me, and helps to put me in the right frame of mind to have an enjoyable, stress-free evening.

INTERMITTENT FASTING

It's time to discuss the benefits of intermittent fasting. Intermittent fasting is defined as any 12-hour period of time (or longer) that the body goes without food. For example, if your last meal is at 6pm and you go to bed and wake up at 6am the next day, your body has been in a "fasting" mode for 12 hours. The keto diet and intermittent fasting go hand in hand to promote a faster weight loss. It's flexible and can be adjusted to suit any lifestyle. As a general rule you should fast for at least 12 hours, but no more than 36 hours. Your body will undergo significant weight loss if you combine keto and intermittent fasting. Both have been shown to balance glucose levels in the bloodstream, improve insulin sensitivity and suppress food cravings. All of this is necessary if your goal is to achieve sustainable weight loss and promote an overall healthier lifestyle. There is a misconception that intermittent fasting limits your calories, but this is not so. Rather, it merely limits your eating window to a specific period of time. Once you have hit your fasting time frame limit, your "eating window" begins, and you can eat any amount of low or zero carb foods you want. Remember that during this eating window the goal is to eat until you are full, but not to "overeat". The good thing about following the keto diet is that overeating is usually not an issue since cravings are generally well controlled when you avoid the carbs and fill up on the healthy fats and proteins instead. If you begin intermittent fasting when you are already restricting carbs, your body reaches ketosis at a quicker rate. Adding the fasting window helps you with the initial phase of your diet, which is usually the most difficult for anyone.

Studies have shown that both ketosis and fasting are healthy for the human brain. When you follow the keto diet, sometime within the first 30 days your body stops depending on glucose. Once it enters the state of ketosis it has begun using stored fat for energy instead, and this state of ketosis is associated with enhanced mental clarity. Intermittent fasting has shown to improve a broad range of neuro-degenerative conditions, including stroke, Huntington's disease, Parkinson's disease, and Alzheimer's disease. Studies conducted at the National Institute on Aging, found that cyclical fasting helps neurons in the brain to resist degeneration and dysfunction.

You'll have to allow some time for your body to get used to skipping meals, or fasting long periods of time between meals. The best way to acclimate your body to this type of eating pattern is to occasionally skip a meal. As your body gets used to going longer periods of time without food, you can move forward with longer fasts. Most people say that skipping breakfast is a great way to get started since your body is already in a "fasting mode" from your hours of sleep.

Many people find that they meet their weight loss goals more quickly if they fast for 20 hours each day and consume their calories in a four-hour window. Remember, this is an ultimate "goal", it's something that can be worked up to gradually. Don't try to rush it – you'll get there. The keto diet is designed to help you learn a new way of eating and to gradually lose excess weight; it's not a race to the finish line. For many, you'll be changing the habits of a lifetime.

It is hard to stumble, when you're on your knees.

SUMMING UP

Pray, do daily bible reading, and get your house in order. Utilize the greatest support system you have going for you – The Holy Trinity. Speak to God, Read His Word, and Listen as the Holy Spirit guides you on your journey to a healthier life.

Follow the suggestions outlined in the book, and develop a Support System of fellow believers if possible. Try to get a group of others interested in losing weight and breaking bad eating habits, those that want to develop a closer walk with God by deepening their devotion and strengthening their personal relationships with Him. If your church agrees, you can start a Keto for Christians Group and hold weekly meetings at the church to discuss your progress, share recipes, and gain strength from one another. Here are some key take-a-ways:

- Begin and end in Prayer each day
- Commit to a daily devotional and Bible Study
- Weigh your food
- Drink water
- Choose quality carbs
- Get enough sleep
- Reduce stress
- Begin light or moderate exercise
- Engage in Intermittent fasting

Above all else, stay in constant prayer and be willing, and ready to forgive any weaknesses, and to start each day anew with the power of positive thinking and a CAN-DO ATTITUDE!

MY PERSONAL EXPERIENCE

My personal keto-diet journey began on June 1, 2018. I was on the return leg of a 24- hour-each-way driving trip from Florida. I felt miserable. I was tired, headachy and in a lot of pain. My feet were so swollen that the skin on my big toe had actually split. The arthritis in my hands was causing both my thumbs to seize up and I couldn't grip the steering wheel. I had cut my visit in Florida short because of the way I had been feeling. I am usually an upbeat, energetic individual who is game for almost any activity. But this time, I could barely walk to go shopping or to eat at a restaurant. My entire body was swollen, my arthritis was at an all-time high pain level, and I felt as though I had the flu. I was nauseous, nervous, and edgy. My head hurt, my back hurt, my legs and feet hurt – actually, it would be easier to list those parts of my body that didn't hurt. I spent the majority of my visit in Florida sitting in my sister's recliner with my feet up.

When I just couldn't take it anymore, I left. I was sad and full of regret, but I felt like I had no choice. I packed up my jeep, loaded in my dog, and hit the road. After 12 hours of driving and filling up on junk-food, I arrived at my oldest son's house (which marks the half-way point for this journey). The pain had escalated, the swelling was worse and all I could think of was getting inside and laying down. I was frustrated, tried of all the pain, I was anxious and irritable and thoughtless. To top it off, my prayers were insincere and selfish. I felt betrayed by my body; forsaken by my God; I simply could not understand why He was allowing this to happen to me, or why, if indeed He was, purposefully putting me through all of this agony. To tell the truth, I was actually a little peeved. That tells you a lot about the frame of mind I was in.

For months I had been slowly slipping into an all too familiar, rather comfortable, secular frame of mind. My human nature took over, and although I said my prayers daily, I did not actually think about what I was saying/praying. It was just routine, a habit. I had let my mind ease back into a thoughtless way of thinking about my relationship with God – in fact, I had stopped thinking about the relationship part at all! I was on auto-pilot. That old time, lazy, daydreaming kind of way. Wake up, say your prayers, read a bible verse, start your day. Just going through the motions. There was no effort, no thought put into my actions – just an off handed need to get these spiritual things over with so I could feel like I had done my duty, and begin my day. I had lost myself, my true self, somewhere along the line. It happened slowly, quietly, and I'm ashamed to say, rather easily. It had actually been like this for months. I'm not sure when it happened, or why. I just know that I had been suffering from a disquieting sense of unease for a very, very long time– out of touch, full of angst and discontented.

This was more or less my mood at the end of this long day, as I pulled into my son's driveway in Brandon Mississippi. The evening air heavy, breezeless and dank, sent me into a river of sweat as soon as I opened my jeep door to get out. Perfect. My mood was now complete.

It was spring break for his kids, and my son's family was away at the beach for a week. It was going to be just he and I for the next two days, and I was looking forward to some "alone" time with my boy. No kids running circles around me, begging me to take them shopping, or to get hamburgers and fries. Just he and I. This thought alone filled my heart with waves of a love that only a mother can understand. My big sweet, cuddly man-cub. I couldn't wait to wrap my arms around him and hug him with all my strength. What a shock when I finally saw him!

My son has always been a large person. He entered this world an amazing 10lb, 21" long baby and never stopped growing. As a child we called him "stocky" and bought him husky sized jeans. He was sweet, lovable, kind, compassionate and always a bit over-weight. Now, 40 years later he was a "big man", six feet tall and around 300lbs. Or at least, he was the last time I had seen him.

This day, as I wearily climbed out of my jeep and went to meet him, instead of the jolly, bigger-than-life man he had always been, was a completely different person. In his place stood a slim, athletic looking man who personified the picture of good health. I was astonished, amazed, and thrilled to see him looking so good – so happy – so healthy!

We spent the next two days discussing his amazing transformation and how he had changed his life with the keto-diet. He talked to me about the food he ate, the weight he had lost, and the mental clarity he had discovered. His self-assurance and positive attitude illuminated his entire being. He was radiant. His testimonial inspired me. The keto diet philosophy made so much sense, and the keto way of eating sounded exactly like what I needed to turn my life around! We discussed the evils of sugar as a whole, and that very day I made a commitment to eliminate sugar from my diet entirely. It was the first step I made towards my new life. I wanted to feel and look as good as he did! I made that one small change and was determined to study and earn everything I could, as fast as I could, about this new way of eating. I was hooked.

I have been struggling with my weight for most of my life. On my 5'2" frame I was currently carrying 218  pounds of weight. It was crushing me. Engulfing my organs; liver, heart, kidneys; the weight was quite literally crushing my knees, my feet and my soul. I had tried many, many diets before, failing each time, my addiction to sugar and sweets an overwhelming obstacle. When I couldn't find a diet that worked, I made up excuses to alleviate my guilt. And I continued to eat. I ate when stressed, I ate when I was upset, I ate for comfort and solace. I ate for pleasure. It was my only vice, I told myself, I deserved this one thing.

I had never looked at my weight problem from a biblical standpoint before. It was one of those things that I had taken for granted as being a part of human nature – a lack of self-control

All those years I never believed it had anything to do with my spirituality, or with growing my relationship with God. I was just fat. That was a normal state of affairs in the United States, and I fit right in with 45% of the population. I accepted it and continued on with my life, enjoying too much of anything edible.

My weight has continued to affect my health in some extremely negative ways. I often had trouble breathing when laying down to sleep at night; I was constantly retaining large amounts of fluid that created inflammation surrounding the joints in my body, causing my arthritis to rage. I'm sure that having a fatty-liver only contributed to my almost constant bouts of nausea and that my never-ending heartburn had a lot to do with my eating habits, or rather, my over-eating habits.

On that particular night in June, another extraordinary thing happened. The excitement of experiencing my son's miraculous transformation changed me. My mind was opened – my soul seemed more awake, more aware.

As I readied for bed and began to pray, I felt a renewed enthusiasm for communicating with God. Finally, after all these months, I was once again ready and able to really listen. The Holy Spirit moved within my soul, and I realized with a clarity I had not known before, that my overeating was a mortal sin. I was desecrating the temple God had given me so generously, poisoning the very body that housed His Holy Spirit. It was a revelation.

God works in mysterious ways, it's true, and He has often used a single event to create life altering consequences. This is what I felt that evening of June 1, 2018 as I knelt to pray in the tiny guest room of my son's house. A single sincere prayer, answered with the gentle whisper of the inspired voice of the Holy Spirit set my soul on a path to seek His Truth. A single thought, brought about by a sincere desire to communicate, was the answer given to me that night.

Being overweight is a sin. The sin is called Gluttony.

A startling realization provided to me as an answered prayer. It was a sin. Literally. I found myself shaking uncontrollably as I sat there on the floor of that quiet room. Suddenly realizing that I had been committing a serious sin almost all of my life. A sudden, overwhelming fear consumed me. I had been committing this sin over and over every day of my life, never once understanding what I was actually doing. Ignorance of the law is no excuse, we have all heard that phase and understand what it means. My ignorance, or lack of clarity was no defense; I could no longer use it as an excuse to continue overeating.

No wonder I had failed at every diet I had attempted – I had attempted them on my own, trying to utilize my own strength, my own wisdom, my own understanding. I had left God out of the equation.

That night I asked forgiveness for having continued in sin for so many years. I asked for wisdom to understand what God had planned for me next, and I committed to shedding the excess pounds plaguing my body and soul, and to make God a major part of the process. I prayed for strength to begin the journey, and I prayed that God would provide the enlightenment I needed to study his Word and discover all He had to tell me about the sin of Gluttony.

If we confess our sins, he is faithful and just and will forgive us our sins and purify us from all unrighteousness. I John 1:9

Every day is a new start. As humans, we are fallible. We are not, and never will be perfect. We will make mistakes, we will fall. We will at times, fail. But for God's grace, we have the ability to shake it off, and begin each day with a fresh start. When we ask, we will be forgiven, our slate wiped clean.

I start and end each day now in prayer for God's guidance on this journey towards good health. I often find myself stopping during the day to pray when I find my will faltering, and I need His strength to carry on. Prayer is Powerful. Prayer is Life Changing.

Losing weight and changing your life, creating and maintaining healthy eating habits is attainable. Through the power of the Holy Spirit, dedication to prayer, and the sincere desire to grow in your relationship with God, all things are possible.

Whenever you doubt yourself, or feel defeated, God will be there to encourage, provide strength, and to help you find forgiveness. You are worthy – you are loved – you are a child of God.

My prayer for you today is that you fall on your knees and sincerely seek the face of God. He alone will make the difference between another failure, or a huge success.

Matthew 19:26 - But Jesus beheld [them], and said unto them, with men this is impossible; but with God all things are possible.

Luke 1:37 - For with God nothing shall be impossible.

Philippians 4:13 - I can do all things through Christ which strengthens me.

MEAL PLANNING

The key to hitting your daily macros and being successful on this diet is to plan, plan, plan. I'm not going to lie, it's not so easy. But with practice and determination anything is possible.

When you fail to plan, you plan to fail. It's that simple. Not planning your diet can easily cause you to be kicked out of ketosis. It is imperative in the first few weeks of your diet to plan your meals to help you avoid excessive snacking or getting involved in binge eating episodes! Dedicated effort to plan your meals will omit the need or temptation to eat foods randomly.

Remember to keep it simple the first week or two. Breakfasts of eggs fried (or scrambled) in butter, several slices of bacon and sliced avocado are best. You can mix it up by using breakfast sausage every other day, or eating just eggs, or just meat items. I prefer to add a little picante sauce or salsa to my eggs for added flavor. There are plenty of easy go-to keto mug breads out there if you prefer a bread for breakfast. My suggestion is that you invest in a keto cookbook with hundreds of recipes to help you on your journey.

Meal planning is a matter of individual tastes, needs, and weight loss goals. You must decide for yourself based on your macro needs how to divide up your daily calories, and what meals mean more to you than the others. Some people prefer a large breakfast while others are just not hungry when they first wake up. Some people may prefer to combine intermittent fasting into their diet and wait until later in the day to eat, so breakfast menus are meaningless to them. You decide.

Once you get the hang of it, you'll be planning your own meals like a pro!

I pray that you find your place, your pace, and your peace on your keto diet journey! The Keto diet is not just a short-term method of weight loss, but a way to reshape the way you think and feel about food. Utilizing this keto book will help you to develop better, healthier eating choices, break bad habits, kick food addictions, and to create a healthier way of eating that you can sustain throughout the rest of your life.

May God bless you, and may your faith increase daily as you continue to renew and strengthen your relationship with Him.

I Chronicles 16:11   Seek the Lord and His strength, seek his face continually.

The

14- Day Meal Plan and Recipes

The Beginners Guide to the

Keto Way of Eating

(WOE)

TWO WEEK MEAL PLANS AND RECIPES

I've provided the following two-week meal plans to help you jump-start your lifestyle change and begin your new Keto Way-of-Eating. I know it's hard in the beginning to know where to start, so I've taken the guess work out! If you find that these meals work well for you, feel free to double them up and use them for the first month of your diet. There's absolutely nothing wrong with repetition in the beginning!

I've also included several other options that you can choose from, or simply add to the plan to create a four- or six-week meal plan. You'll note however, that the additional menus do not have the macros calculated. This was done deliberately to challenge you to learn to calculate the macros on your own.

You'll need to calculate your own personal macros to determine what calorie range you need to stay in, then adjust these meals to fit your needs. So be sure to check an on-line keto macro calculator to find out how many calories you need. You can always omit some portion of these foods if you need to eat less calories, and on the flip side, you can always add extra ingredients while cooking if you need to consume more calories, or throw in a snack or two during the day.

Remember, in order to succeed, you have to plan. Read through the recipes before you begin and create a shopping list to ensure you have everything you need on hand. This one simple task will help to make sure you have a successful two weeks!

A note of caution: be sure to check each recipe for any ingredients you may have a known allergy to and substitute for another low-carb ingredient.

WEEK ONE MEAL PLAN AND RECIPES

Here are the meals and recipes for the first week on your Keto Diet. Feel free to add snacks throughout when you find yourself still hungry. Olives, avocados, nuts and seeds are great high-fat snacks. Just watch your serving size on the nuts as the carbs can add up quickly! A handful of nuts is NOT a serving size!

DAY 1:

BREAKFAST:

Almond Flour Pancakes

430 calories: 39g fat: 14g carbs: 12g protein: 4g fiber

INGREDIENTS:

1/4 cup almond flour
1 organic egg
2 tbsp softened coconut oil

1 tsp coconut oil
Stevia to taste (or another sweetener of choice)

DIRECTIONS:

1. Make the batter by cracking the egg and whisk it with the melted 2 tbsp coconut oil, mixing well. Stir in the almond flour and stevia. The batter will be a little thicker than normal pancake mix.

2. Heat the pan over medium heat with coconut oil.

3. Drop some batter onto the pan the size of a pancake you'd want. When the bubbles start showing up on top flip the pancake and cook for another minute. Repeat if needed until done.

LUNCH:

Sirloin Steak Salad with Avocado

454 calories: 35g fat: 8g carbs: 23g protein: 3g fiber

INGREDIENTS:

4 oz sirloin steak (fatty cut)
1/4 avocado, peeled and diced
1/8 tsp freshly ground black pepper
1 tsp lemon juice
1 cup salad greens

6 grape tomatoes, halved
1 tbsp organic coconut oil
1/8 tsp sea salt
1 tsp extra virgin olive oil

DIRECTIONS:

1. Melt coconut oil on a nonstick pan over medium heat. Rub the steak with salt and pepper
2. Cook the steak in the skillet until done, about 4 minutes per side.
3. Remove the steak and let cool for about 5 minutes.
4. In a medium bowl, combine salad greens, tomato and avocado. Add lemon juice and olive oil. Toss
5. Slice the steak and serve on top of salad. Enjoy!

DINNER:

Baked Mustard Pork Chop (makes 2 servings, nutrition facts are for one (1) serving)

285 calories: 20g fat :6g carbs: 24g protein: 1g fiber

INGREDIENTS:

2 (4 oz each) Pork Chops   2 tsp garlic powder
6 oz Dijon Mustard   2 tbsp organic coconut oil
2 tsp dried thyme   2 cup broccoli florets

DIRECTIONS:

1. Preheat oven to 425°F.
2. Rinse the pork chops and season with salt and pepper. Set aside.
3. Blend mustard, thyme and crushed garlic. Pour over the pork chops and coat each side.
4. Heat up an oven-proof pan with 1 tbsp coconut oil, brown the pork chops and transfer to the oven. Cook for another 5-8 minutes.
5. Sauté the broccoli in the remaining 1 tbsp coconut oil.
6. Serve broccoli and pork chop together.

DAY 2:

BREAKFAST:

Yogurt, Berries and Nuts

266 calories:14g fat: 11g carbs: 2g protein: 5g fiber

INGREDIENTS:

8 oz Plain unsweetened coconut
yogurt
1/4 cup fresh raspberries
1/4 cup chopped walnuts

DIRECTIONS:

1. Add yogurt to a bowl.
2. Sprinkle the berries and nuts on top. ENJOY!

LUNCH:

Baked Mustard Pork Chop (leftovers)

285 calories: 20g fat: 6g carbs: 24g protein: 1g fiber

INGREDIENTS:

2 (4 oz each) Pork Chops	2 tsp garlic powder
6 oz Dijon Mustard	2 tbsp organic coconut oil
2 tsp dried thyme	2 cup broccoli florets

DIRECTIONS:

1. Preheat oven to 425° F.

3. Rinse the pork chops and season with salt and pepper. Set aside.
4. Blend mustard, thyme and crushed garlic. Pour over the pork chops and coat each side.
5. Heat up an oven-proof pan with 1 tbsp coconut oil, brown the pork chops and transfer to the oven. Cook for another 5-8 minutes.
6. Sauté the broccoli in the remaining 1 tbsp coconut oil.
7. Serve broccoli and pork chop together.

DINNER:

Zucchini and Ground Beef

468 calories: 35g fat: 8g carbs: 28g protein: 2g fiber

INGREDIENTS:

5 oz ground beef
1 medium zucchini
1/2 tsp chili powder
1/8 tsp salt

1/8 tsp pepper
1 tbsp Extra Virgin olive oil
2 Tbsp lemon juice

DIRECTIONS:

1. Brown the beef in oil, stirring frequently. Once the beef is cooked, add the sliced zucchini. Stir.
2. Season with chili powder, salt and pepper. Cook for a few minutes. Turn off the heat.
3. Drizzle with lemon juice and serve.

DAY 3:

<u>**BREAKFAST:**</u>

Bacon Egg Cups (makes 4 cups, 2 cups per serving)

200 calories: 13g fat: 2g carbs: 16g protein: 0g fiber

INGREDIENTS:

4 eggs
4 slices bacon

DIRECTIONS:

1. Preheat oven to 350°F and grease muffin pan.
2. Cook bacon until almost done.
3. Put one slice of bacon into each hole of muffin pan and then split an egg on each one.
4. Bake for 10 minutes for semi, soft yolk. Cook under 10 minutes for runny yolk and more than 10 minutes for hard egg.
5. NOTE: SAVE 1/2 THE RECIPE FOR *LEFTOVERS* ON FRIDAY!!

<u>**LUNCH:**</u>

Arugula, Bacon and Walnut Salad

271 calories: 24g fat: 3g carbs: 8g protein: 2g fiber

INGREDIENTS:

2 cups arugula
3 bacon slices, diced
1 tbsp chopped walnuts

1 tbsp organic extra virgin olive oil
1/2 tbsp lemon juice

DIRECTIONS:

1. Cook bacon over high heat until crispy.
2. Remove bacon, dice it and place in a bowl with arugula.
3. Add 1 tbsp of olive oil in the pan and add walnuts, stirring until lightly roasted.
4. Combine walnuts with arugula and bacon. Add lemon juice. Toss and serve.

DINNER:

Sausage Stuffed Peppers (makes 2 peppers – save one for lunch the next day – nutritional facts are for 1 (one) stuffed pepper)

326 calories: 20g fats: 21g carbs: 19g protein: 7g fiber

INGREDIENTS:

6 oz ground Italian hot sausage	1/2 yellow onion
2 Green Bell Peppers	2 clove garlic
1 1/2 cup cauliflower rice	1 tsp dried thyme
2 oz tomato paste	

DIRECTIONS:

1. Heat oven to 350°F. Cut off the tops of peppers and remove the seeds, wash and drain.
2. Grate the cauliflower, resembling rice consistency. Place cauliflower rice in a bowl, put in spices and herbs, minced garlic and onion. Set aside.
3. Heat up a pan with oil and sear the sausage, once done add to the bowl of cauliflower, add the tomato paste. Mix well.
4. Stuff the peppers with the mixture. Place in oven and cook 40 min. Enjoy.

DAY 4:

BREAKFAST:

Strawberry Coconut Smoothie

131 calories: 10g fat: 11g carbs: 4g protein: 5g fiber

INGREDIENTS:

6 strawberries
1/2 cup canned coconut milk
2 tbsp walnuts

DIRECTIONS:

Blend and enjoy!

LUNCH:

Sausage Stuffed Pepper

326 calories: 20g fats: 21g carbs: 19g protein: 7g fiber

INGREDIENTS:

4 Bell peppers	1 can Rotel
8 ounces cream cheese	Olive Oil
1 pound Italian sausage	Pinch Red Pepper Flakes

DIRECTIONS:

1. Cut bell peppers in half and remove the seeds.
2. After cleaning the inside out, drizzle with olive oil and bake in oven at 350°F for 25 – 35 minutes or until tender.

3. While the peppers are baking, break the sausage up and brown.
4. Add can of rotel without draining the grease.
5. Add softened cream cheese and stir until melted.
6. Add crushed red pepper to taste.
7. Remove peppers from oven, stuff them with the sausage mixture and return to oven. Bake for 5-10 minutes more.
8. Serve warm.

DINNER:

Chicken with Olives and Tomatoes (makes 2 servings – nutritional facts are for one serving)

504 calories: 41g fat: 11g carbs: 20g protein: 4g fiber

INGREDIENTS:

6 oz chicken breast
4 tbsp organic Extra Virgin olive oil
2 tbsp lemon juice
1/4 tsp salt
2 tsp thyme

1/4 tsp pepper
2 clove garlic
1/2 yellow onion, chopped
12 grape tomatoes
30 kalamata olives

DIRECTIONS:

1. Marinate chicken cutlets in a mixture of 1 tbsp olive oil, lemon juice, salt and pepper for an hour.
2. Preheat oven to 375° F. Grease a baking dish.
3. Sauté sliced onions and garlic in remaining tbsp oil, stir. Add tomatoes and olives, stir. Add thyme.
4. Put marinated chicken into the baking dish, add the sautéed veggies. Cover and bake for 40 minutes. Enjoy.

DAY 5:

<u>**BREAKFAST:**</u>

Quick Broccoli Scramble

268 calories: 15g fat: 4g carbs: 13g protein: 1g fiber

INGREDIENTS:

2 eggs
1/4 cup broccoli florets, finely
chopped
1 tbsp coconut oil

DIRECTIONS:

1. Break the eggs into the bowl and press the egg yolk to break.
2. Mix the broccoli with the eggs.
3. Add coconut oil to pan and turn on heat to medium to melt.
4. Pour the eggs mixture into the frying pan. Scramble until set. Sprinkle salt and pepper as desired.

<u>**LUNCH:**</u>

Avocado Cucumber Soup

266 calories: 30g fat: 19g carbs: 6g protein: 11g fiber

INGREDIENTS:

1 avocado
1 small cucumber
1/2 cup water

1 tbsp lemon juice
1/8 tsp salt
1 clove garlic

DIRECTIONS:

1. Halve the avocado, peel and remove the seed. Reserve 1/4 of the flesh and dice. Put the rest in a food processor or blender.
2. Peel and chop the cucumber, add to the avocado in the food processor.
3. Add the water, cumin, garlic, lemon and salt. Puree until smooth.
4. Transfer into a serving dish, place the reserved avocado on top.
   *serve cold or warm in microwave for hot soup.

DINNER:

Thai Coconut Soup (makes two servings

434 calories: 46g fat: 9g carbs: 21g protein: 0g fiber

INGREDIENTS:

12 oz beef broth	1/8 tsp sea salt
1/2 cup canned coconut milk	3 oz sirloin steak, chopped
1/8 tsp dried chili flakes	1 tbsp organic coconut oil
1/2 tsp ginger	1 tbsp fresh basil (chopped)
1/4 cup lemon juice	

DIRECTIONS:

1. Melt the coconut oil in a pan, add the beef. Cook for 4 minutes. Add the rest of the ingredients and bring to a boil. Lower heat, simmer for 20 minutes.
2. Toss with chopped basil, stir. Enjoy.

DAY 6:

BREAKFAST:

Bacon Egg Cups

200 calories: 13g fat: 2g carbs: 16g protein: 0g fiber

INGREDIENTS:

4 eggs   4 slices bacon

DIRECTIONS:

1. Preheat oven to 350°F and grease muffin pan.
2. Fry bacon until almost done.
3. Put one slice of bacon into each hole of muffin pan and then split an egg on each one.
4. Bake for 10 minutes for semi, soft yolk. Cook under 10 minutes for runny yolk and more than 10 minutes for hard egg.

LUNCH:

Thai Coconut Soup

434 calories: 46g fat: 9g carbs: 21g protein: 0g fiber

INGREDIENTS:

12 oz beef broth   1/8 tsp sea salt
1/2 cup canned coconut milk 3 oz sirloin steak, chopped
1/8 tsp dried chili flakes   1 tbsp organic coconut oil
1/2 tsp ginger   1 tbsp fresh basil (chopped)
1/4 cup lemon juice

DIRECTIONS:

1. Melt the coconut oil in a pan, add the beef. Cook for 4 minutes. Add the rest of the ingredients and bring to a boil. Lower heat, simmer for 20 minutes.
2. Toss with chopped basil, stir. Enjoy.

DINNER:

50-50 Burgers (this recipe makes 2 servings; nutrition facts are for one (1) serving)

510 calories: 43g fat: 6g carbs: 26g protein: 3g fiber

INGREDIENTS:

6 oz grass fed ground beef
4 oz nitrate free bacon, chopped finely
1/2 TBSP paprika

1/2 tbsp garlic powder
1/4 tbsp ground black pepper
1 bunch asparagus, chopped
1 tbsp organic coconut oil

DIRECTIONS:

1. Put the meat in a mixing bowl, add all the spices and shape into patties.
2. Grill each side for about 6 minutes, or until cooked.
3. Sauté the asparagus in the oil. Serve together.
4. NOTE: SAVE 1/2 THE RECIPE FOR *LEFTOVERS* TOMORROW!!

DAY 7:

<u>**BREAKFAST:**</u>

Yogurt, Berries and Seeds

158 calories: 12g fat: 11g carbs: 3g protein: 5g fiber

INGREDIENTS:

4 oz Plain unsweetened coconut
yogurt
6 strawberries (sliced)
2 tbsp roasted sunflower seeds

DIRECTIONS:

1. Add yogurt to a bowl.
2. Sprinkle the berries and seeds on top. ENJOY!

<u>**LUNCH:**</u>

50-50 Burgers

510 calories: 43g fat: 6g carbs: 26g protein: 3g fiber

INGREDIENTS:

6 oz ground beef
4 oz bacon, chopped finely
1/2 tbsp paprika
1/2 tbsp garlic powder

1/4 tbsp ground black pepper
1 bunch asparagus, chopped
1 tbsp organic coconut oil

DIRECTIONS:

1. Put the meat in a mixing bowl, add all the spices and shape into patties.
2. Grill each side for about 6 minutes, or until cooked.
3. Sauté the asparagus in the oil. Serve together.

DINNER:

Chicken with Olives and Tomatoes

504 calories: 41g fat: 11g carbs: 20g protein: 4g fiber

INGREDIENTS:

6 oz chicken breast	1/4 tsp pepper
4 tbsp Extra Virgin olive oil	2 clove garlic
2 tbsp lemon juice	1/2 yellow onion, chopped
1/4 tsp salt	12 grape tomatoes
2 tsp thyme	30 kalamata olives

DIRECTIONS:

1. Marinate chicken cutlets in the mixture of 1 tbsp olive oil, lemon juice, salt and pepper for an hour.
2. Preheat oven to 375° F. Grease a baking dish.
3. Sauté sliced onions and garlic in remaining tbsp oil, stir. Add tomatoes and olives, stir. Add thyme.
4. Put marinated chicken into the baking dish, add the sautéed veggies. Cover and bake for 40 minutes. Enjoy.

WEEK TWO MEAL PLAN AND RECIPES

Here are the recipes for Week Two on your Keto Diet. Feel free to add snacks throughout when you find yourself still hungry. Olives, avocados, nuts and seeds are great high-fat snacks. Just watch your serving size on the nuts as the carbs can add up quickly! Check the labels for serving sizes.

DAY 1:

Breakfast

Scrambled Eggs with Buttered Basil

Calories 427: Fat 42g: Protein 13g: Carbs 3g

INGREDIENTS:

2 ounces butter
4 eggs
4 tbsp coconut cream or coconut milk or sour cream

4 tbsp fresh basil
Salt to taste

DIRECTIONS:
1. Place a non-stick pan on low heat and melt butter.
2. In a small bowl, whisk eggs, coconut cream, basil and salt. Pour into hot pan
3. With a spatula, stir eggs until scrambled and cooked to desired doneness.
4. Serve warm, or place in meal prep container to save for later.

Lunch:

Chicken-Avocado Lettuce Wraps

Calories 264: Fat 20g: Protein 12g: Carbs 9g: Fiber 3g

INGREDIENTS:

½ avocado, peeled and pitted
1/3 cup mayonnaise
1 tsp freshly squeezed lemon
juice
2 tsp chopped fresh thyme

1 (6-ounce) cooked chicken
breast, chopped
Sea salt
Freshly ground black pepper
8 large lettuce leaves
¼ cup chopped walnuts

DIRECTIONS:

1. In a medium bowl, mash the avocado with the mayonnaise, lemon juice, and thyme until well combined.
2. Stir in the chopped chicken and season the filling with the salt and pepper.
3. Spoon the chicken salad into the lettuce leaves and top with the walnuts.
4. Serve 2 lettuce leaves per person.

Dinner:

Baked Coconut Haddock

Calories 299: Fat 24g: Protein 20g: Carbs 1g

INGREDIENTS:

4 (5 oz) boneless haddock fillets	1 cup shredded unsweetened coconut
Sea salt	½ cup ground hazelnuts
Freshly ground pepper	2 tbsp coconut oil, melted

DIRECTIONS:

1. Preheat the oven to 400°F. Line a baking sheet with parchment paper and set aside.
2. Pat the fillets dry with paper towels and lightly season the with salt and pepper.
3. Stir together the shredded coconut and hazelnut in a small bowl.
4. Dredge the fish fillets in the coconut mixture so that both sides of each piece are thickly coated.
5. Place the fish on the baking sheet and lightly brush both sides of each piece with the coconut oil.
6. Bake the haddock until the topping is golden and the fish flakes easily with a fork, about 12 minutes total.
7. Serve.

DAY 2:

<u>**Breakfast:**</u>

Nut medley Granola

Calories 391: Fat 38g: Protein 10g: Carbs 10 g

INGREDIENTS

2 cups shredded unsweetened coconut
1 cup sliced almonds
1 cup raw sunflower seeds
½ cup raw pumpkin seeds

½ cup walnuts
½ cup melted coconut oil
10 drips liquid Stevia
1 tsp ground cinnamon
½ tsp ground nutmeg

DIRECTIONS:

1. Preheat the oven to 250 degrees. Line 2 baking sheets with parchment paper. Set aside.
2. Toss together the shredded coconut, almonds, sunflower seeds, pumpkin seeds, and walnuts in a large bowl until mixed.
3. In a small bowl, stir together the coconut oil, stevia, cinnamon, and nutmeg until blended
4. Pour the coconut oil mixture into the nut mixture and use your hands to blend until the nuts are well coated.
5. Transfer the granola mixture to the baking sheet and spread it out evenly.
6. Bake the granola, stirring every 10 to 15 minutes until the mixture is golden brown and crunchy, about 1 hour.
7. Transfer the granola to a large bowl and let the granola cool, tossing it frequently to break up the large pieces.
8. Store the granola in airtight containers in the refrigerator or freezer for up to 1 month.

Lunch:

Crab Salad-Stuffed Avocado

Calories 389: Fat 31g: Protein 19g: Carbs 10g

INGREDIENTS:

1 avocado, peeled, halved lengthwise
½ tsp freshly squeezed lemon juice
4 ½ ounces crabmeat
½ cup cream cheese
¼ cup chopped red bell pepper

¼ cup chopped, peeled cucumber
½ scallion, chopped
1 tsp chopped cilantro
Freshly ground black pepper
Pinch of sea salt

DIRECTIONS:

1. Brush the cut edges of the avocado with the lemon juice and set the halves aside on a plate.
2. In a medium bowl, stir together the crabmeat, cream cheese, red pepper, cucumber, scallion, cilantro, salt and pepper until well mixed.
3. Divide the crab mixture between the avocado halves and store them, covered with plastic wrap, in the refrigerator until you are ready to serve them, up to 2 days

Dinner:

CHICKEN BACON BURGERS

Calories 374: Fat 33g: Protein 18g: Carbs 3g

INGREDIENTS:

1 pound ground chicken
8 bacon slices, chopped
1/3 cup ground almonds
1 tsp chopped fresh basil
¼ tsp sea salt

Pinch freshly ground black
pepper
2 tbsp coconut oil
4 large lettuce leaves
1 avocado, peeled, pitted and
sliced

DIRECTIONS:

1. Preheat the oven to 350°F. Line a baking sheet with parchment paper and set aside.
2. In a medium bowl, combine the chicken, bacon, ground almonds, basil, salt, and pepper until well mixed.
3. Form the mixture into 6 equal patties.
4. Place a large skillet over medium-high heat and add the coconut oil.
5. Pan sear the chicken patties until brown on both sides, about 6 minutes in total.
6. Place the browned patties on the baking sheet and bake until completely cooked through, about 15 minutes.
7. Serve on lettuce leaves, topped with the avocado slices.

DAY 3:

Breakfast:

Peanut Butter Cup Smoothie

Calories 486: Fat 40g: Protein 30 g: Carbs 6 g

INGREDIENTS:

1 cup water
¾ cup coconut cream
1 scoop chocolate protein powder

2 tbsp natural peanut butter
3 ice cubes

DIRECTIONS:

1. Put the water, coconut cream, protein powder, peanut butter and ice in a blender and blend until smooth.
2. Pour into 2 glasses and serve immediately.

Lunch:

BLT Salad

Calories 228: Fat 18g: Protein 1g: Carbs 4g

INGREDIENTS:

2 tbsp melted bacon fat
2 tbsp red wine vinegar
Freshly ground black pepper
4 cups shredded lettuce
1 tomato, chopped
6 bacon slices, cooked and chopped

2 hardboiled eggs, chopped
1 tbsp roasted unsalted sunflower seeds
1 tsp toasted sesame seeds
1 cooked chicken breast, sliced

DIRECTIONS:

1.   In a medium bowl, whisk together the bacon fat and vinegar until emulsified. Season with black pepper,
2.   Add the lettuce and tomato to the bow and toss the vegetables with the dressing.
3.   Divide the salad between 4 plates and top each with equal amounts of bacon, egg, sunflower seeds, sesame seeds and chicken. Serve.

Note: you can choose to eliminate the chicken if you prefer a simple BLT flavor. If you want to try a warm bacon salad dressing, gently warm the bacon fat before whisking in the vinegar. Swap out the regular lettuce for kale or spinach; the more robust greens will hold up better in the dressing.

Dinner:

Baked Salmon with Almonds and Cream Sauce

Calories 522: Fat 44g: Protein 28g: Carbs 2.4g

INGREDIENTS:

Almond Crumbs Creamy Sauce	Fish
3 tbsp shaved almonds	1 salmon fillet (about ½ lb.)
2 tbsp almond milk (for thinning the sauce if necessary)	1 tsp coconut oil
	1 tbsp lemon zest
½ cup cream cheese	1 tsp salt
Salt to taste	White pepper to taste

DIRECTIONS:

1. Prepare the salmon: cut the salmon in half. Mix the lemon zest, salt and pepper together and rub the mixture on the salmon. Let it stand in the refrigerator for 20 minutes so the seasonings will be absorbed. Meanwhile, preheat the oven to 300°F.

2. Heat some coconut oil on a nonstick baking dish. Fry the fish on both sides for a few minutes and make sure that the fish is sealed. Top with almond crumbs and bake in the oven for 10 to 15 minutes.

3. Take the dish out of the oven and transfer the fish to a separate plate. Set aside.

4. Place the baking dish on a fire and add the cream cheese. Combine the fish baking juices and the cheese for a more flavorful sauce.

5. Mix well until uniformed. If necessary, add some almond milk to the sauce.

6. Pour the sauce onto the fish. Best served hot.

DAY 4:

<u>**Breakfast:**</u>

Avocado and Eggs

Calories 324: Fat 25g: Protein 19g: Carbs 8g

INGREDIENTS:

2 avocados, peeled, halved lengthwise
4 large eggs
1 (4 oz) chicken breast, cooked and shredded

¼ cup Cheddar cheese
Sea salt
Freshly ground pepper

DIRECTIONS:

1. Preheat the oven to 425°F
2. Take a spoon and hollow out each side of the avocado halves until the hole is about twice the original size.
3. Place the avocado halves in an 8-by-8-inch baking dish, hollow side up.
4. Crack an egg into each hollow and divide the shredded chicken between each avocado half. Sprinkle the cheese on top of each and season lightly with the salt and pepper.
5. Bake the avocados until the eggs are cooked through, about 15 to 20 minutes.
6. Serve immediately.

Lunch:

Cauliflower-Cheddar Soup

Calories 227: Fat 21g: Protein 8g: Carbs 4g: Fiber 2g

INGREDIENTS:

¼ cup butter	½ tsp ground nutmeg
½ sweet onion	1 cup heavy (whipping) cream
1 head cauliflower	Sea salt
4 cups Herbed Chicken stock	Freshly ground black pepper
	1 cup shredded Cheddar cheese

DIRECTIONS:

1. Put a large stockpot over medium heat and add the butter.
2. Sauté the onion and cauliflower until tender and lightly browned.
3. Add the chicken stock and nutmeg to the pot and bring the liquid to a boil.
4. Reduce the heat to low and simmer until the vegetables are very tender, about 15 minutes.
5. Remove the pot from the heat, stir in the heavy cream, and puree the soup with an immersion blender or food processor until smooth.
6. Season the soup with salt and pepper and serve topped with the Cheddar cheese.

Dinner:

Baked Fish Fillets with Vegetables in Foil

Calories 339: Fat 19g: Protein 35g: Carbs 4.7g

INGREDIENTS:

1 lb. cod (or any white fish)
1 red bell pepper, sliced
6 cherry tomatoes, halved
1 leek (small size, only the white part, sliced)
¼ onion, sliced
½ zucchini, sliced

1 clove garlic, chopped
2 tbsp olives
1 oz butter
2 tbsp olive oil
½ lemon sliced to taste
Coriander leaves, to taste (optional)
Salt and pepper to taste

DIRECTIONS:

1. Preheat oven to 400°F.
2. Slice the zucchini, leek, onion, bell pepper and lemon, cut tomatoes in half, chop the garlic.
3. Transfer all the vegetables to a baking sheet lined with foil.
4. Cut the fish into bite-sized pieces and add to the vegetables. Add salt and pepper, drizzle olive oil and add pieces of butter around evenly.
5. Fold the foil and make sure you seal the joints of the foil well
6. Bake for 35 – 40 minutes
7. Can be served with aioli or any other low carb sauce of your choice.

DAY 5:

Breakfast:

Low-Carb Crepe

Calories 162: Fat 14.2 g: Protein 7.7g: Carbs 1.1g

INGREDIENTS:

Batter	Topping
2 oz cream cheese (full fat)	½ cup mixed berries
2 eggs	2 tsp heavy whipping cream

DIRECTIONS:

1. Warm up cream cheese in a microwave so it gets soft and easy to mix
2. Add 2 eggs to cream cheese (one at a time) and mix well. Use a hand blender or a whisk. Add any spices to the mixture (optional)
3. Warm up a skillet, oil it slightly and make your crepes.
4. Optional: You can make it sweet by adding whipped cream, strawberries, berries, Greek yogurt, maple syrup and cinnamon. (Make sure it fits your macros.)

Lunch:

Cauliflower-Cheddar soup

Calories 227: Fat 21g: Protein 8g: Carbs 4g: Fiber 2g

INGREDIENTS:

¼ cup butter
½ sweet onion
1 head cauliflower
4 cups Herbed Chicken stock

½ tsp ground nutmeg
1 cup heavy (whipping) cream
Sea salt
Freshly ground black pepper
1 cup shredded Cheddar cheese

DIRECTIONS:

1. Put a large stockpot over medium heat and add the butter.
2. Sauté the onion and cauliflower until tender and lightly browned.
3. Add the chicken stock and nutmeg to the pot and bring the liquid to a boil.
4. Reduce the heat to low and simmer until the vegetables are very tender, about 15 minutes.
5. Remove the pot from the heat, stir in the heavy cream, and puree the soup with an immersion blender or food processor until smooth.
6. Season the soup with salt and pepper and serve topped with the Cheddar cheese.

Dinner:

Roasted Pork Loin with Grainy Mustard Sauce and Mushrooms with Camembert

Calories 368: Fat 29g: Protein25g: Carbs 2g

INGREDIENTS:

1 (2pound) boneless pork loin roast
Sea Salt
Freshly ground black pepper

3 tbsp olive oil
1 ½ cups heavy (whipping) cream
3 tbsp grainy mustard (such as Pommery)

DIRECTIONS:

1. Preheat the oven to 375°F.
2. Season the port loin all over with sea salt and pepper
3. Place a large skillet over medium-high heat and add the olive oil.
4. Brown the roast on all sides in the skillet, about 6 minutes in total, and place the roast in a baking dish.
5. Roast until a meat thermometer inserted in the thickest part of the roast reads 155°F, about 1 hour.
6. When there is approximately 15 minutes of roasting time left, place a small saucepan over medium heat and add the heavy cream and mustard.
7. Stir the sauce until it simmers, then reduce the heat to low. Simmer the sauce until it is very rich and thick, about 5 minutes. Remove the pan from the heat and set aside.
8. Let the pork rest for 10 minutes before slicing and serve with the sauce.

DAY 6:

Breakfast Egg Bake

Calories 303: Fat24 g: Protein 17 g: Carbs 4 g

INGREDIENTS:

1 tbsp olive oil, plus extra for greasing the casserole dish
1 pound sausage
8 large eggs
2 cups cooked spaghetti squash

1 tbsp chopped fresh oregano
Sea salt
Freshly ground black pepper
½ cup shredded Cheddar cheese

DIRECTIONS:

1. Preheat the oven to 375°F. Lightly grease a 9-by-13-inch casserole dish with olive oil and set aside.
2. Place a large ovenproof skillet over medium-heat and add the olive oil.
3. Brown the sausage until cooked through, about 5 minutes. While the sausage is cooking, whisk together the eggs, squash, and oregano in a medium bowl. Season lightly with salt and pepper and set aside.
4. Add the cooked sausage to the egg mixture, stir until just combined, and pour the mixture into the casserole dish.
5. Sprinkle the top of the casserole with the cheese and cover the casserole loosely with aluminum foil.
6. Bake the casserole for 30 minutes, and then remove the foil and bake for another 15 minutes.
7. Let the casserole stand for 10 minutes before serving.

Lunch:

Roasted Pork Loin with Grainy Mustard Sauce

Calories 368: Fat 29g: Protein25g: Carbs 2g

INGREDIENTS:

1 (2pound) boneless pork loin roast
Sea Salt
Freshly ground black pepper

3 tbsp olive oil
1 ½ cups heavy (whipping) cream
3 tbsp grainy mustard (such as Pommery)

DIRECTIONS:

1. Preheat the oven to 375°F.
2. Season the port loin all over with sea salt and pepper.
3. Place a large skillet over medium-high heat and add the olive oil.
4. Brown the roast on all sides in the skillet, about 6 minutes in total, and place the roast in a baking dish.
5. Roast until a meat thermometer inserted in the thickest part of the roast reads 155°F, about 1 hour.
6. When there is approximately 15 minutes of roasting time left, place a small saucepan over medium heat and add the heavy cream and mustard.
7. Stir the sauce until it simmers, then reduce the heat to low. Simmer the sauce until it is very rich and thick, about 5 minutes. Remove the pan from the heat and set aside.
8. Let the pork rest for 10 minutes before slicing and serve with the sauce.

Dinner:

Lemon Butter Chicken

Calories 294: Fat 26g: Protein 12g: Carbs3g

INGREDIENTS:

4 bone-in, skin-on chicken thighs
Sea salt
Freshly ground black pepper
2 tbsp butter, divided
2 tsp minced garlic

½ cup Herbed chicken stock
½ cup heavy (whipping) cream
Juice of ½ lemon

DIRECTIONS:

1. Preheat oven to 400°F.
2. Lightly season the chicken thighs with salt and pepper.
3. Place a large ovenproof skillet over medium-high heat and add 1 tablespoon of butter.
4. Brown the chicken thighs until golden on both sides, about 6 minutes in total. Remove the thighs to a plate and set aside.
5. Add the remaining 1 tablespoon of butter and sauté the garlic until translucent, about 2 minutes.
6. Whisk in the chicken stock, heavy cream and lemon juice
7. Bring the sauce to a boil and then return the chicken to the skillet.
8. Place the skillet in the oven, covered, and braise until the chicken is cooked through, about 30 minutes.

DAY 7:

Breakfast:

Keto Pancakes with Sugar-Free-Syrup and Scrambled Eggs

Calories 78: Protein 2.5 g: Carbs 1.5g

INGREDIENTS:

3 tbsp coconut flour	1 tsp baking powder
3 tbsp sour cream	1 tsp vanilla extract
¼ cup butter softened	1 tbsp powdered sweetener
4 eggs	¼ cup water

DIRECTIONS:

1. Combine all dry ingredients in a medium-sized bowl. Mix well and set aside.
2. In a large mixing bowl, combine sour cream with butter, vanilla extract, and water. Mix on high for 2 minutes. Add eggs, one at a time, beating constantly.
3. Add dry ingredients and continue to mix for 3 minutes.
4. Grease a non-stick skillet with oil and heat over medium-high heat.
5. Using a large spoon, pour batter into skillet and cook for 2 minutes or until bubbles disappear. Flip and continue to cook for one more minute.
6. Serve immediately.

Lunch:

BLT SALAD

Calories 228: Fat 18g: Protein 1g: Carbs 4g

INGREDIENTS:

2 tbsp melted bacon fat	2 hardboiled eggs, chopped
2 tbsp red wine vinegar	1 tbsp roasted unsalted
Freshly ground black pepper	sunflower seeds
4 cups shredded lettuce	1 tsp toasted sesame seeds
1 tomato, chopped	1 cooked chicken breast, sliced
6 bacon slices, cooked and chopped	

DIRECTIONS:

1. In a medium bowl, whisk together the bacon fat and vinegar until emulsified. Season with black pepper.
2. Add the lettuce and tomato to the bowl and toss the vegetables with the dressing.
3. Divide the salad between 4 plates and top each with equal amounts of bacon, egg, sunflower seeds, sesame seeds and chicken. Serve.

Note: you can choose to eliminate the chicken if you prefer a simple BLT flavor. If you want to try a warm bacon salad dressing, gently warm the bacon fat before whisking in the vinegar. Swap out the regular lettuce for kale or spinach; the more robust greens will hold up better in the dressing.

Dinner:

PAPRIKA CHICKEN

Calories 389: Fat 30g: Protein 25g: Carbs 4g

INGREDIENTS:

4 (4oz) chicken breasts
Sea slat
Freshly ground black pepper
1 tsp olive oil
½ cup chopped sweet onion

½ cup heavy (whipping) cream
2 tsp smoked paprika
½ cup sour cream
2 tbsp chopped fresh parsley

DIRECTIONS:

1. Lightly season the chicken with salt and pepper.
2. Place a large skillet over medium-high heat and add the olive oil.
3. Sear the chicken on both sides until almost cooked through, about 15 minutes in total. Remove the chicken to a plate.
4. Add the onion to the skillet and sauté until tender, about 4 minutes.
5. Stir in the cream and paprika and bring the liquid to a simmer.
6. Return the chicken and any accumulated juices to the skillet and simmer the chicken for 5 minutes until completely cooked.
7. Stir in the sour cream and remove the skillet from the heat.
8. Serve topped with the parsley.

MENU NOTES

If at any time during these first two weeks you feel hungry after eating, you can add snacks as long as you make sure you don't exceed your daily macros. I've provided a section specifically for snacks on the following pages. Satisfy your cravings, and appease your appetite with these nutritious, keto-friendly snack ideas!

If you are one of those people that just can't eat first thing in the morning, feel free to substitute a Smoothie for any breakfast (or lunch or dinner item for that matter) on any day. You'll find several optional smoothie recipes in the following pages.

Understanding your own personal macro needs is imperative on the keto-diet. You'll need to familiarize yourself with macro-calculators, determine your daily goals, and then create your own daily (or weekly) mean plans. This will most likely be the most challenging part of your keto journey. Learning to read labels to gauge true carb counts, applying nutritional information to your favorite recipes, and becoming so familiar with it all you can do it in your sleep!

To help you with this task, I've provided a few "sample" meal plans for you to practice on! These menus are keto-friendly and should meet the needs of almost everyone's macro needs. But it's your turn to figure them out!

As an added bonus, I've included a number of recipes that are my personal favorites for you to try. I hope you enjoy them as much as I do.

Don't worry. In the beginning we don't worry that much about limiting calories; so if you have trouble with the macros, just use your My Fitness Pal app (or whatever app you decide on) and plug in the 5%, 25% and 70% percentiles and you will be good to go.

MONDAY

Breakfast: scrambled egg lettuce-wrap with avocado and cilantro
Snack: nuts
Lunch: kale salad with grilled chicken and olive oil dressing
Snack: bell pepper with guacamole
Dinner: steak with cauliflower rice

TUESDAY

Breakfast: baked egg in an avocado cup
Snack: Macadamia nuts
Lunch: tuna salad with a side of green salad
Snack: sliced cheese or cold cut turkey roll-ups
Dinner: Chinese Beef and broccoli

WEDNESDAY

Breakfast: full-fat Greek yogurt topped with chia seeds and crushed walnuts
Snack: Turkey jerky (look for "no sugar added")
Lunch: cauliflower fried rice
Snack: sliced cheese
Dinner: roast beef with sautéed mushroom and zucchini

THURSDAY

Breakfast: blackberry protein shake with kale and almond butter
Snack: zucchini parmesan chips

Lunch: chicken tenders made with almond flour on a bed of greens with cucumbers and cheese
Snack: bacon deviled eggs
Dinner: grilled shrimp topped with a lemon butter sauce with a side of asparagus

FRIDAY

Breakfast: Fried eggs with bacon and a side of greens
Snack: ½ cup coconut chips
Lunch: Burger in a lettuce "bun" topped with avocado and a side salad
Snack: Celery sticks dipped in almond butter
Dinner: Meatloaf on a bed of watercress salad

SATURDAY

Breakfast: Feta Cheese and spinach omelet
Snack: bacon wrapped asparagus
Lunch: chicken wings with celery sticks
Snack: cocoa coconut milk smoothie
Dinner: Grilled chicken with bell peppers and tomatoes

SUNDAY

Breakfast: full-fat Greek yogurt with coconut and pumpkin seeds
Snack: cheese crisp
Lunch: chicken salad wraps
Snack: Peanut butter fat bombs
Dinner: grilled salmon with a side of cauliflower rice

MONDAY

Breakfast: 3 egg omelet with spinach, cheese, and sausage.
Lunch: BLT Salad
Dinner: Baked Salmon with Asparagus

TUESDAY

Breakfast: Bacon and Eggs

Lunch: Spinach Salad

Dinner: Cheese-Stuffed Bunless Burgers

WEDNESDAY

Breakfast: Egg muffins
Lunch: Cottage Cheese, Walnuts, and Hot Sauce (substitute blueberries if preferred)
Dinner: Meatloaf with spinach salad

THURSDAY

Breakfast: Sausage links, scrambled eggs
Lunch: Tuna salad lettuce wraps
Dinner: Chicken wings with Ranch Dressing dipping sauce

FRIDAY

Breakfast: Avocado-Baked Eggs
Lunch: Chicken and Hummus Lettuce Wraps
Dinner: Philly Cheesesteak Casserole

SATURDAY

Breakfast: Bullet proof coffee
Lunch: Sliced ham and cheese lettuce wraps with mayo
Dinner: Steak and broccoli

SUNDAY

Breakfast: Keto Pancakes with sugar free syrup
Lunch: Tuna Salad sandwich on keto mug bread
Dinner: Kielbasa with green bell pepper and sautéed onions

RECIPES

Alternative Keto recipes for everyday use

BREAKFAST AND SMOOTHIES

Scrambled Eggs with Buttered Basil

Breakfast Bake

Nut Medley Granola

Almond Blueberry Muffins

Keto Pancakes

Avocado and Eggs

Mushroom Frittata

Bacon-Artichoke Omelet

Low-Carb Crepe

Cinnamon Almond Butter Smoothie

Bulletproof Chocolate Smoothie

Strawberry Avocado Smoothie

Peanut Butter Cup Smoothie

Berry Green Smoothie

Scrambled Eggs with Buttered Basil

Serves 2 / Prep Time: 5 minutes / Cook Time: 15 minutes

INGREDIENTS:

2 ounces butter
4 eggs
4 tbsp coconut cream or
coconut milk or sour cream

4 tbsp fresh basil
Salt to taste

DIRECTIONS:

1. Place a non-stick pan on low heat and melt butter.
2. In a small bowl, whisk eggs, coconut cream, basil and salt. Pour into hot pan.
3. With a spatula, stir eggs until scrambled and cooked to desired doneness.
4. Serve warm, or place in meal prep container to save for later.

Per Serving: Calories 427: Fat 42g: Protein 13g: Carbs 3g

Breakfast Bake

Serves 8 / Prep time: 10 minutes / Cook time: 50 minutes

INGREDIENTS:

1 tbsp olive oil, plus extra for greasing the casserole dish
1 pound sausage
8 large eggs
2 cups cooked spaghetti squash

1 tbsp chopped fresh oregano
Sea salt
Freshly ground black pepper
½ cup shredded Cheddar cheese

DIRECTIONS:

1. Preheat the oven to 375. Lightly grease a 9-by-13 inch casserole dish with olive oil and set aside.
1. Place a large ovenproof skillet over medium-heat and add the olive oil.
2. Brown the sausage until cooked through, about 5 minutes. While the sausage is cooking, whisk together the eggs, squash, and oregano in a medium bowl. Season lightly with salt and pepper and set aside.
3. Add the cooked sausage to the egg mixture, stir until just combined, and pour the mixture into the casserole dish.
4. Sprinkle the top of the casserole with the cheese and cover the casserole loosely with aluminum foil.
5. Bake the casserole for 30 minutes, and then remove the foil and bake for another 15 minutes.
6. Let the casserole stand for 10 minutes before serving

Per serving: Calories 303: Fat24g: Protein 17g: Carbs 4g

Nut Medley Granola

Serves 8 / Prep time: 10 minutes / Cook time: 1 hour

INGREDIENTS:

2 cups shredded unsweetened coconut
1 cup sliced almonds
1 cup raw sunflower seeds
½ cup raw pumpkin seeds

½ cup walnuts
½ cup melted coconut oil
10 drips liquid Stevia
1 tsp ground cinnamon
½ tsp ground nutmeg

1. Preheat the oven to 250 degrees. Line 2 baking sheets with parchment paper. Set aside.
2. Toss together the shredded coconut, almonds, sunflower seeds, pumpkin seeds, and walnuts in a large bowl until mixed.
3. In a small bowl, stir together the coconut oil, stevia, cinnamon, and nutmeg until blended.
4. Pour the coconut oil mixture into the nut mixture and use your hands to blend until the nuts are well coated.
5. Transfer the granola mixture to the baking sheets and spread it out evenly.
6. Bake the granola, stirring every 10 to 15 minutes until the mixture is golden brown and crunchy, about 1 hour.
7. Transfer the granola to a large bowl and let the granola cool, tossing it frequently to break up the large pieces.
8. Store the granola in airtight containers in the refrigerator or freezer for up to 1 month.

Per serving: Calories 391: Fat 38g: Protein 10g: Carbs 10g

Almond Blueberry Muffins

Serves 10 / Prep time: 10 minutes / Cook time: 17 minutes

INGREDIENTS:

2 eggs
1 cup fresh blueberries
¼ cup Flaxseed Meal
½ cup Almond slices
1 tbsp almond butter
½ cup Unsweetened almond milk

1 cup almond flour
1 tbsp baking powder
2 tbsp butter (melted)
1 tbsp Olive oil
1/3 cup Sweetener
1 tsp Vanilla extract

DIRECTIONS:

1. While preheating the oven to 350°F, beat 2 eggs and sweetener in a mixing bowl for around 5 minutes until the mixture becomes light and airy.
2. Put the baking powder, almond four, almond butter, almond milk, and the flaxseed meal in the egg mixture. Then pour the melted butter, the vanilla extract, and the olive oil. Stir the ingredients together.
3. Gently drop the shaved almonds and fresh blueberries into the mixture and fold.
4. Prepare a muffin or cupcake pan and transfer the batter into it. Top with additional shaved almonds.
5. Bake for 17 minutes or until the muffins are cooked thoroughly.
6. Remove from the oven and enjoy.

Per muffin: Calories 167: Fat 14 g: Protein 5.6g: Carbs 3.6g

Keto Pancakes

Servings: 12 / Prep Time 5 minutes / Cook time 5 minutes

INGREDIENTS:

3 tbsp coconut flour	1 tsp baking powder
3 tbsp sour cream	1 tsp vanilla extract
¼ cup butter softened	1 tbsp powdered sweetener
4 eggs	¼ cup water

DIRECTIONS:

1. Combine all dry ingredients in a medium-sized bowl. Mix well and set aside.
2. In a large mixing bowl, combine sour cream with butter, vanilla extract, and water. Mix on high for 2 minutes. Add eggs, one at a time, beating constantly.
3. Add dry ingredients and continue to mix for 3 minutes.
4. Grease a non-stick skillet with oil and heat over medium-high heat.
5. Using a large spoon, pour batter into skillet and cook for 2 minutes or until bubbles disappear. Flip and continue to cook for one more minute.
6. Serve immediately.

Per Serving: Calories 78: Protein 2.5g: Carbs 1.5g

Avocado and Eggs

Servings: 4 / Prep Time: 10 minutes / Cook time: 20 minutes

INGREDIENTS

2 avocados, peeled, halved lengthwise

4 large eggs

1 (4 oz) chicken breast, cooked and shredded

¼ cup Cheddar cheese

Sea salt

Freshly ground pepper

DIRECTIONS:

1. Preheat the oven to 425°F.
2. Take a spoon and hollow out each side of the avocado halves until the hole is about twice the original size.
3. Place the avocado halves in an 8-by-8-inch baking dish, hollow side up.
4. Crack an egg into each hollow and divide the shredded chicken between each avocado half. Sprinkle the cheese on top of each and season lightly with the salt and pepper.
5. Bake the avocados until the eggs are cooked through, about 15 to 20 minutes.
6. Serve immediately.

Per Serving: Calories 324: Fat 25g: Protein 19g: Carbs 8g

Mushroom Frittata

Serves 6 / Prep time: 10 minutes / Cook time: 15 minutes

INGREDIENTS:

2 tbsp olive oil
1 cup sliced fresh mushrooms
1 cup shredded spinach
6 bacon slices, cooked and chopped

10 large eggs, beaten
½ cup crumbled goat cheese
Sea salt
Freshly ground black pepper

DIRECTIONS:

1. Preheat the oven to 350°F.
2. Place a large ovenproof skillet over medium-high heat and add the olive oil.
3. Sauté the mushrooms until lightly browned, about 3 minutes.
4. Add the spinach and bacon and sauté until the greens are wilted, about 1 minute.
5. Add the eggs and cook, lifting the edges of the frittata with a spatula so uncooked egg flows underneath, for 3 to 4 minutes.
6. Sprinkle the top with the crumbled goat cheese and season lightly with salt and pepper.
7. Bake until set and lightly browned, about 15 minutes.
8. Remove the frittata from the oven, and let stand for 5 minutes.
9. Cut into 6 wedges and serve immediately.

Per serving: Calories 316: Fat 27g: Protein16g: Carbs 1g

Bacon-Artichoke Omelet

Serves 4 / Prep time: 10 minutes / Cook time: 10 minutes

INGREDIENTS:

6 eggs, beaten
2 tbsp heavy(whipping) cream
8 bacon slices, cooked and
chopped
1 tbsp olive oil

¼ cup chopped onion
½ cup chopped artichoke
hearts (canned, packed in
water)
Sea Salt
Freshly ground black pepper

DIRECTIONS:

1. In a small bowl, whisk together the eggs, heavy cream, and bacon until well blended and set aside.
2. Place a large skillet over medium-high heat and add the olive oil.
3. Sauté the onion until tender, about 3 minutes.
4. Pour the mixture into the skillet, swirling it for 1 minute.
5. Cook the omelet, lifting the edges with a spatula to let the uncooked egg flow underneath, for 2 minutes.
6. Sprinkle the artichoke hearts on top and flip the omelet. Cook for 4 minutes more, until the egg is firm. Flip the omelet over again so the artichoke hearts area on top.
7. Remove from the heat, cut the omelet into quarters, and season with salt and black pepper.
8. Serve while hot.

Per serving: Calories 435: Fat 39g: Protein 17g: Carbs 5g

Low-Carb Crepe

Servings 2 / Prep time: 5 minutes / Cook time: 10 minutes

INGREDIENTS:

Batter
2 oz cream cheese (full fat)
2 eggs

Topping
½ cup mixed berries
2 tsp heavy whipping cream

DIRECTIONS:

1. Warm up cream cheese in a microwave so it gets soft and easy to mix.
2. Add 2 eggs to cream cheese (one at a time) and mix well. Use a hand blender or a whisk. Add any spices to the mixture (optional).
3. Warm up a skillet, oil it slightly (I put some oil on a bounty and wiped my skillet) and make your crepes.
4. Optional: You can make it sweet by adding whipped cream, strawberries, berries, Greek yogurt, maple syrup and cinnamon. (Make sure it fits your macros.)

Per serving: Calories 162: Fat 14.2g: Protein 7.7g: Carbs 1.1g

Cinnamon Almond Butter Smoothie

Servings: 1 / Prep Time 5 minutes / Cook time 2 minutes

INGREDIENTS:

1 ½ cups unsweetened nut milk   15 drops liquid stevia
1 scoop collagen peptides   1/8 tsp almond extract
2 tbsp almond butter   1/8 tsp salt
½ tsp cinnamon   6-8 ice cubes

DIRECTIONS:

1. Add all the ingredients to a blender and combine for 30
    seconds or until you get a smooth consistency.

Per Serving: Calories 326: Fats 27g: Protein 19g: Carbs 11g

Bulletproof Chocolate Smoothie

Servings 2 / Prep time: 3 minute / Cook time: 2 minutes

INGREDIENTS:

1 ¼ cup fresh brewed coffee, cooled for at least 15 minutes
¼ cup filtered water

2 scoops Chocolate Collagen Protein Powder
6-8 Ice cubes

DIRECTIONS:

1. Blend coffee, water and chocolate protein powder until smooth, adding ice cubes until you reach desired consistency.
2. Serve immediately in a glass with a straw.

Per serving: Calories 30: Fat 0g: Protein 0g: Carbs less than 1g

Basic Bulletproof Coffee Drink

Servings 1 / Prep time: 2 minutes / Cook time: 1 minute

INGREDIENTS:

1 cup brewed coffee
1 tsp coconut oil
1 tbsp butter, unsalted

¼ tsp vanilla extract
A few drops of stevia

DIRECTIONS:

1. Put all ingredients into blender. Mix on high for 20 seconds until frothy.
2. Drink immediately.

Per serving: Calories 148: Protein 0g: Fat 14g: Carbs less than 1

Strawberry Avocado Green Smoothie

Servings: 1-2 / Prep time: 5 minutes / Cook time: 5 minutes

INGREDIENTS:

1 cup fresh strawberries, hulled

½ medium, ripe avocado, peeled

1 cup (packed) baby spinach

1 cup unsweetened almond milk

2 teaspoons sweetener

6-8 ice cubes

DIRECTIONS:

1. Place all ingredients into blender and blend until smooth.
2. Once blended, taste for sweetness and adjust accordingly by adding more strawberries or sweetener as needed.
3. Serve immediately.

Per serving: Calories 156: Fat 6.9 g: Protein 2.7g: Carbs 6.9g

Peanut Butter Cup Smoothie

Servings 2 / Prep time 5 Minutes

INGREDIENTS:

1 cup water
¾ cup coconut cream
1 scoop chocolate protein
powder

2 tablespoons natural peanut
butter
3 ice cubes

DIRECTIONS:

1. Put the water, coconut cream, protein powder, peanut
   butter and ice in a blender and blend until smooth.
2. Pour into 2 glasses and serve immediately.

Per serving: Calories 486: Fat 40g: Protein 30g: Carbs 6g

Berry Green Smoothie

Servings: 2 / Prep time 10 minutes

You might be taken aback by the unusual color of this smoothie – it's kind of greenish brown- but the taste is similar to raspberry cheesecake. Kale is a perfect addition to smoothies because it has a less assertive taste than some other greens. Kale is also a spectacular source of vitamin K and very high in vitamins A and C.

INGREDIENTS:

1 cup water	¾ cup cream cheese
½ cup raspberries	1 tablespoon coconut oil
½ cup shredded kale	1 scoop vanilla protein powder

DIRECTIONS:

1. Put the water, raspberries, kale, cream cheese, coconut oil and protein powder in a blender and blend until smooth.
2. Pour into 2 glasses and serve immediately.

Per serving: Calories 436: Fat 36g: Protein 28g: Carbs 6g

Spinach-Blueberry Smoothie

Serves 2 / Prep time: 5 minutes

Blueberries are the second most popular berry in the United States and have one of the highest antioxidant contents of any food. Throwing a handful of this fruit in your morning smoothie adds vitamins K and C, magnesium, and copper to your diet. Look for organic berries because they have a higher antioxidant level than conventionally grown fruit.

INGREDIENTS:

1 cup coconut milk

1 cup spinach

½ cucumber, chopped

½ cup blueberries

1 scoop plain protein powder

2 tbsp coconut oil

4 ice cubes

Mint sprigs for garnish

DIRECTIONS:

1. Put the coconut milk, spinach, cucumber, blueberries, protein powder, coconut oil, and ice into a blender and blend until smooth.
2. Pour into 2 glasses, garnish each with the mint, and serve immediately.

Per serving: Calories 353: Fat 32g: Protein 15g: Carbs6g

APPITIZERS AND SNACKS

Queso Dip

Crab Salad-Stuffed Avocado

Chicken-Avocado Lettuce Wraps

BLT Salad

Cauliflower-Cheddar Soup

Bacon-Cheese Deviled Eggs

Crispy Parmesan Crackers

Parmesan Crisps with Tomato Slices

Onion Cheese Muffins

Cheesy Cauliflower Breadsticks

Bacon Flavored Kale Chips

Keto-approved Trail Mix

Cheese Roll-Ups

Bacon & Cheddar Cheese Balls

Queso Dip

Serves 6 / Prep Time: 5 minutes / Cook time: 10 minutes

INGREDIENTS:

½ cup coconut milk
½ jalapeno pepper, seeded and diced
1 tsp minced garlic
½ tsp onion powder

2 ounces goat cheese
6 ounces sharp Cheddar cheese, shredded
¼ tsp cayenne pepper

DIRECTIONS:

1. Place a medium pot over medium heat and add the coconut milk, jalapeno, garlic, and onion powder.
2. Bring the liquid to a simmer and then whisk in the cheese until smooth.
3. Add the Cheddar cheese and cayenne and whisk until the dip is thick, 30 seconds to 1 minute.
4. Pour into a serving dish and serve with keto crackers or low-carb veggies.

Per serving: Calories 213: Fat 19g: Protein 10g: Carbs 2g

Crab Salad-Stuffed Avocado

Servings: 2 / Prep time: 20 minutes

Be sure to get real crab meat and not the imitation product. If you do choose to use frozen, be sure to thaw it completely and squeeze out any extra liquid so that your salad isn't soggy.

INGREDIENTS:

1 avocado, peeled, halved lengthwise
4 ½ ounces crabmeat
½ cup cream cheese
¼ cup chopped red bell pepper
½ scallion, chopped
¼ cup chopped, peeled cucumber
1 tsp chopped cilantro
Freshly ground black pepper
Pinch of sea salt
½ tsp freshly squeezed lemon juice

DIRECTIONS:

1. Brush the cut edges of the avocado with the lemon juice and set the halves aside on a plate.
2. In a medium bowl, stir together the crabmeat, cream cheese, red pepper, cucumber, scallion, cilantro, salt and pepper until well mixed.
3. Divide the crab mixture between the avocado halves and store them, covered with plastic wrap, in the refrigerator until you are ready to serve them, up to 2 days.

Per serving: Calories 389: Fat 31g: Protein 19g: Carbs 10g

Chicken-Avocado Lettuce Wraps

Serves 4 / Prep time: 10 minutes

Substituting lettuce wraps for the bread is a spectacular way of enjoying your favorite sandwiches while avoiding all those unhealthy carbs. The best lettuce to use is Boston, large red or green oak leaf, or romaine lettuce with the rib cut out. Cutting out the rib allows you to roll the lettuce leaf without it cracking or ripping.

INGREDIENTS:

½ avocado, peeled and pitted
½ cup creamy Mayonnaise
1 tsp freshly squeezed lemon juice
2 tsp chopped fresh thyme
8 large lettuce leaves

1 6-ounce cooked chicken breast, chopped
Sea Salt
Freshly ground black pepper
¼ cup chopped walnuts

DIRECTIONS:

1. In a medium bowl, mash the avocado with the mayonnaise, lemon juice and thyme until well combined.
2. Stir in the chopped chicken and season the filling with salt and pepper.
3. Spoon the chicken salad into the lettuce leaves and top with the walnuts.
4. Serve 2 lettuce wraps per person.

Per serving: Calories 264: Fat 20g: Protein 12g: Carbs 9g

BLT Salad

Serves 4 / Prep time: 15 minutes

INGREDIENTS:

2 tbsp melted bacon fat
2 tbsp red wine vinegar
Freshly ground black pepper
4 cups shredded lettuce
1 tomato, chopped
6 bacon slices, cooked and chopped

2 hardboiled eggs, chopped
1 tbsp roasted unsalted sunflower seeds
1 tsp toasted sesame seeds
1 cooked chicken breast, sliced

DIRECTIONS:

1. In a medium bowl, whisk together the bacon fat and vinegar until emulsified. Season with black pepper.
2. Add the lettuce and tomato to the bow and toss the vegetables with the dressing.
3. Divide the salad between 4 plates and top each with equal amounts of bacon, egg, sunflower seeds, sesame seeds and chicken. Serve.

Note: you can choose to eliminate the chicken if you prefer a simple BLT flavor. If you want to try a warm bacon salad dressing, gently warm the bacon fat before whisking in the vinegar. Swap out the regular lettuce for kale or spinach; the more robust greens will hold up better in the dressing.

Per serving: Calories 228: Fat 18g: Protein 1g: Carbs 4g

Cauliflower-Cheddar Soup

Serves 8 / Prep time: 10 minutes / Cook time: 30 minutes

INGREDIENTS:

¼ cup butter
½ sweet onion
1 head cauliflower
4 cups Herbed Chicken stock
½ tsp ground nutmeg

1 cup heavy (whipping) cream
Sea salt
Freshly ground black pepper
1 cup shredded Cheddar
cheese

DIRECTIONS:

1. Put a large stockpot over medium heat and add the butter.
2. Sauté the onion and cauliflower until tender and lightly browned.
3. Add the chicken stock and nutmeg to the pot and bring the liquid to a boil.
4. Reduce the heat to low and simmer until the vegetables are very tender, about 15 minutes.
5. Remove the pot from the heat, stir in the heavy cream, and puree the soup with an immersion blender or food processor until smooth.
6. Season the soup with salt and pepper and serve topped with the Cheddar cheese.

Per serving: Calories 227: Fat 21g: Protein 8g: Carbs 4g

Bacon-Cheese Deviled Eggs

Makes 12 / Prep time: 15 minutes

INGREDIENTS:

6 large eggs, hardboiled and peeled

¼ cup mayonnaise

¼ avocado, chopped

½ tsp Dijon mustard

¼ cup swiss cheese, finely shredded

6 Bacon slices, cooked and chopped

Freshly ground black pepper

DIRECTIONS:

1. Halve each of the eggs lengthwise.
2. Carefully remove the yolk and place the yolks in a medium bowl. Place the whites, hollow-side up, on a plate.
3. Mash the yolks with a fork and add the mayonnaise, avocado, cheese, and Dijon mustard. Stir until well mixed. Season the yolk mixture with the black pepper.
4. Spoon the yolk mixture back into the egg while hollows and top each egg half with the chopped bacon.
5. Store the eggs in an airtight container in the refrigerator for up to 1 day.

PREP TIP: Hardboiled eggs make perfect snacks and a great addition to many recipes such as salads and entrees. Hard-boil a dozen eggs at the beginning of the week and keep them in the refrigerator for when you need them.

Per serving: Calories 85: Fat 7g: Protein 6g: Carbs 2g

Crispy Parmesan Crackers

Makes 8 crackers / Prep time: 10 minutes / Cook time: 5 minutes

Parmesan cheese has a nice keto ratio, especially when combined with a little butter to create these lacy beauties. The cheese spreads out and melts into large crispy golden crackers that will satisfy any craving for a rich savory treat. You can use grated parmesan as well, as long as it is freshly grated.

INSTRUCTIONS:

1 teaspoon butter   8 ounces full-fat Parmesan cheese, shredded or freshly grated

DIRECTIONS:

1. Preheat oven to 400°F.
2. Line a baking sheet with parchment paper and lightly grease the paper with the butter.
3. Spoon the Parmesan cheese onto the baking sheet in mounds, spread evenly apart.
4. Spread out the mounds with the back of a spoon until they are flat.
5. Bake the crackers until the edges are browned and the centers are still pale, about 5 minutes.
6. Remove the sheet from the oven, and remove the crackers with a spatula to paper towels. Lightly blot the tops with additional paper towels and let them completely cool.
7. Store in a sealed container in the refrigerator for up to 4 days.

Per serving: Calories 133: Fat 11g: Protein 11g: Carbs 1g

Keto Parmesan Crisps with Tomato Slices

Serves 3   / Prep time: 5 minutes / Cook time: 7 minutes

INGREDINTS:

5 tbsp (100 g) Parmesan
freshly grated
1/8 tsp chili powder, to taste

1/8 tsp black pepper, to taste
½ small tomato, thinly sliced

DIRECTIOS:

1. Preheat oven to 390°F and grate Parmesan on the small-hole side of your grater.
2. Mix with chili powder and black pepper.
3. On baking paper, put 1 tablespoon of the mix and gently spread it. Repeat until you have no more parmesan left.
4. Bake for 5 minutes (approximately) the parmesan chips are incredibly quick to bake.
5. Slice half of the tomato in very thin slices and put them on top of the crisps. Bake for 2 more minutes
6. Let them cook for 5 minutes. Enjoy!

Per serving: Calories 147: Fat 10g: Protein 13g: Carbs 2g

Onion Cheese Muffins

Servings 4: Prep time: 10 minutes / Cook time:

This snack is super easy to prep and can be made for breakfast, or a quick snack.   These flavors work together perfectly and also make a great crowd-pleasing appetizer.

INSTRUCTIONS:

¼ cup Colby jack cheese, shredded
¼ cup shallots, minced
1 cup almond flour

1 egg
3 tbsp melted butter
3 tbsp sour cream
½ tsp salt

DIRECTIONS:

1. Line 6 muffin tins with 6 muffing liners. Set aside and preheat oven to 350°F.
2. In a bowl, stir the dry and wet ingredients alternately. Mix well using a spatula until the consistency of the mixture becomes even.
3. Place the batter into the prepared muffin tins.
4. Bake for 20 minutes in oven until golden brown.
5. Let it cook and store in an airtight container.

Per serving: Calories 193: Fat 17.4g: Protein 6.3g: Carbs 5g: Fiber 2g

CHEESY CAULIFLOWER BREADSTICKS

Serves 4   / Prep time: 10 minutes / Cook time: 15 minutes

INGREDIENTS:

1 cauliflower, small head

1 tbsp butter

2 eggs

1 tsp rosemary

1 tsp oregano

2 Cloves garlic, minced

1 tbsp almond flour

1 ½ cups mozzarella cheese

Salt and pepper to taste

DIRECTIONS:

1. Wash and dry the cauliflower thoroughly. Discard the leaves and chop into small florets.
2. Transfer to a food processor and pulse gently to obtain rice-size bits.
3. Put the cauliflower bits in a heat-safe bowl together with a tablespoon of butter. Microwave for 1 minute 30 seconds.
4. Mix the cauliflower rice, almond flour, rosemary, oregano, eggs and a cup of mozzarella cheese in a bowl. Using a spoon to stir well until combined.   Adjust the flavor with salt and pepper.
5. Transfer the mixture to a ~~waxed paper~~ parchment-paper covered baking tray. Pat evenly on all sides.
6. Lay the remaining half cup of mozzarella cheese on top to cover the surface.
7. Leave in the oven set at 300°F for 15 -30 minutes. Baking time may vary depending on how dry/moist you like your topping.
8. Remove from the oven once the cheese turns golden in color. Let stand for 5 minutes to cool then remove from the paper.
9. Cut into slices, serve.

Per Serving: Calories 217: Fat 16g: Protein 14g: Carbs 4g

Bacon-Flavored Kale Chips

Serving Size: 6 / Prep time: 10 minutes / Cook time: 25 minutes

INGREDIENTS:

1 pound kale, around 1 bunch   2 tablespoons butter
1 to 2 teaspoons salt   ¼ cup bacon grease

DIRECTIONS:

1.   Remove the rib from kale leaves and tear into 2-inch pieces.
2.   Clean the kale leaves thoroughly and dry them inside a salad spinner.
3.   In a skillet, add the butter to the bacon grease and warm the two fats over low heat. Add the salt and stir constantly.
4.   Set aside and let it cool.
5.   Put the dried kale in a Ziploc bag and add the cool liquid bacon grease and butter mixture.
6.   Seal the Ziploc bag and gently shake the kale leaves with the butter mixture. The leaves should have the shiny consistency which means that they are coated evenly with the fat.
7.   Pour the kale leaves on a cookie sheet and sprinkle more salt if necessary.
8.   Bake for 25 minutes inside a preheated 350°F oven or until the leaves start to turn brown as well as crispy.
9.   Let it cool, evenly divide into suggested servings and store in an airtight container.

Per Serving: Calories 148: Fat 13g: Carbs 6g: Protein 6g

KETO-APPROVED TRAIL MIX

Serving per recipe: 8 / Cook time: 3 minutes

Quick, easy and nutritious this snack is sure to become an all-time favorite!

INSTRUCTIONS:

½ cup salted pumpkin seeds
½ cup slivered almonds
¾ cup roasted pecan halves

¾ cup unsweetened cranberries
1 cup toasted coconut flakes, unsweetened

DIRECTIONS:

1. In a skillet, place almonds and pecans. Heat for 2-3 minutes and let cool.
2. Once cooled, in a large re-sealable plastic bag, combine all ingredients.
3. Seal and shake vigorously to mix.
4. Evenly divide into suggested servings and store in airtight container.

Per serving: Calories 184: Fat 14g: Protein 4g: Carbs 13g

FISH AND POULTRY

Tuna Stuffed Avocados

Cheesy Garlic Salmon

Herb Butter White Fish

Baked Fish Fillets

Fish & Chips

Baked Salmon with Almonds and Creamy Sauce

Shrimp & Sausage Bake

Herb Butter Scallops

Pan-Seared Halibut with Citrus Butter Sauce

Baked Coconut Haddock

Lemon Butter Chicken

Paprika Chicken

Stuffed Chicken Breasts

Coconut Chicken

Buffalo Drumsticks with Chili Aioli

Baked Fish Fillets with Vegetables in Foil

Serves 3 / Prep time: 10 minutes   / Cook time: 40 minutes

INGREDIENTS:

1 lb. cod (or any white fish)
1 red bell pepper, sliced
6 cherry tomatoes, halved
1 leek (small size, only the white part, sliced)
¼ onion, sliced
½ zucchini, sliced

1 clove garlic, chopped
2 tbsp olives
1 oz butter
2 tbsp olive oil
½ lemon sliced to taste
Coriander leaves, to taste (optional)
Salt and pepper to taste

DIRECTIONS:

1. Preheat oven to 400°F.
2. Slice the zucchini, leek, onion, bell pepper and lemon, cut tomatoes in half, chop the garlic.
3. Transfer all the vegetables to a baking sheet lined with foil.
4. Cut the fish into bite-sized pieces and add to the vegetables. Add salt and pepper, drizzle olive oil and add pieces of butter around evenly.
5. Fold the foil and make sure you seal the joints of the foil tightly.
6. Bake for 35 – 40 minutes.
7. Can be served with aioli or any other low carb sauce of your choice.

Per servings: Calories 339: Fat 19g: Protein 35g: Carbs 5g

Fish & Chips

Servings 2 / Prep time:15 minutes / Cook time: 30 minutes

For chips:
½ tbsp olive oil
1 medium zucchini
Salt and pepper to taste

For Sauce:
2 tbsp dill pickle relish
¼ tbsp curry powder
½ cup mayonnaise

For fish:
¾ lb. cod (or any white fish)
Oil for frying
½ cup almond flour
¼ tsp onion powder

½ tsp paprika powder
½ cup parmesan cheese, grated
1 egg
Salt and pepper to taste

DIRECTIONS:

1. For the sauce, simply combine all the sauce ingredients in a bowl. Mix well and then set aside.
2. Line some parchment paper on a baking sheet and preheat oven to 400°F. Make thin zucchini rods, brush them with oil, and spread them on the baking sheet. Add a pinch of salt and pepper on top. Bake for about 30 minutes or wait until the zucchini turns golden brown.
3. While baking the zucchini, crack the egg in a bowl and beat thoroughly.
4. On a separate plate, combine the parmesan cheese, almond flour, and the remaining spices.
5. Slice the fish into 1 inch by 1-inch pieces. Roll them on the flour mixture. Dip in the beaten egg and sprinkle more flour to cover the pieces again.

6. Place a deep saucepan on the heat with about 340-360°F. Heat the oil for a while, then fry the fish for three minutes on each side. Remove from the heat when it becomes golden brown but make sure that the fish is cooked through.
7. Transfer to a serving plate and serve with the baked Zucchini fries and tartar sauce. You can also use any other keto-friendly sauce of your choice.

Per serving: Calories 463: Fat 26.2 g: Protein 49g: Carbs 6g

Baked Salmon with Almonds and Cream Sauce

Serves 2 / Prep time: 10 minutes / Cook time: 20 minutes

INGREDIENTS:

Almond Crumbs Creamy Sauce	Fish
3 tbsp shaved almonds	1 salmon fillet (about ½ lb.)
2 tbsp almond milk (for thinning	1 tsp coconut oil
the sauce if necessary)	1 tbsp lemon zest
½ cup cream cheese	1 tsp salt
Salt to taste	White pepper to taste

DIRECTIONS:

1. Prepare the salmon: cut the salmon in half. Mix the lemon zest, salt and pepper together and rub the mixture on the salmon. Let it cook in the refrigerator for 20 minutes so the seasonings will be absorbed. Meanwhile, preheat the oven to 300°F.

2. Heat some coconut oil on a nonstick baking dish. Fry the fish on both sides for a few minutes and make sure that the fish is sealed. Top with almond crumbs and bake in the oven for 10 to 15 minutes.

3. Take the dish out of the oven and transfer the fish to a separate plate. Set aside.

4. Place the baking dish on a fire and add the cream cheese. Combine the fish baking juices and the cheese for a more flavorful sauce.

5. Mix well until uniformed. If necessary, add some almond milk to the sauce.

6. Pour the sauce onto the fish. Best served hot.

Per serving: Calories 522: Fat 44g: Protein 28g: Carbs 2.4g

Shrimp and Sausage Bake

Serves 4 / Prep time: 15 minutes / Cook time: 20 minutes

INGREDIENTS:

2 tbsp olive oil
6 ounces chorizo sausage, diced
½ pound (16 to 20 count) shrimp, peeled and deveined
½ small sweet onion, chopped
1 tsp minced garlic
¼ cup Herbed Chicken Stock
Pinch red pepper flakes
1 red bell pepper, chopped

INGREDIENTS:

1. Place a large skillet over medium-high heat and add the olive oil.
2. Sauté the sausage until it is warmed through, about 6 minutes.
3. Add the shrimp and sauté until it is opaque and just cooked through, about 4 minutes.
4. Remove the sausage and shrimp to a bowl and set aside.
5. Add the red pepper, onion, and garlic to the skillet and sauté until tender, about 4 minutes.
6. Add the chicken stock to the skillet along with the cooked sausage and shrimp.
7. Bring the liquid to a simmer and simmer for 3 minutes.
8. Stir in the red pepper flake and serve.

Per serving: Calories 323: Fat 24g: Protein 20g: Carbs 6g

Herb Butter Scallops

Serves 4 / Prep time: 10 minutes / Cook time: 10 minutes

INGREDIENTS:

1 pound sea scallops, cleaned
Freshly ground black pepper
8 tbsp butter, divided
2 tsp minced garlic

Juice of 1 lemon
2 tsp chopped fresh basil
1 tsp chopped fresh thyme

DIRECTIONS:

1. Pat the scallops dry with paper towels and season them lightly with pepper.
2. Place a large skillet over medium heat and add 2 tablespoons of butter.
3. Arrange the scallops in the skillet, evenly spaced but not too close together and sear each side until they are golden brown, about 2 ½ minutes per side.
4. Remove the scallops to a plate and set aside.
5. Add the remaining 6 tablespoons of butter to the skillet and sauté the garlic until translucent, about 3 minutes.
6. Stir in the lemon juice, basil and thyme and return the scallops to the skillet, turning to coat them in the sauce.
7. Serve immediately.

Per serving: Calories 306: Fat 24g: Protein 19g: Carbs 4g

Pan Seared Halibut with Citrus Butter Sauce

Serves 4 / Prep time: 10 minutes / Cook time: 15 minutes

INGREDIENTS:

4 (5 oz) halibut fillets, 1 inch thick
Sea salt
Freshly ground pepper
¼ cup butter
2 tbsp minced garlic
1 shallot, minced

3 tablespoons dry white wine
1 tbsp freshly squeezed orange juice
1 tbsp freshly squeezed lemon juice
2 tsp chopped fresh parsley
2 tsp olive oil

DIRECTIONS:

1. Pat the fish dry with paper towels and then lightly season the fillets with salt and pepper. Set aside on a paper towel-lined plate.
2. Pace a small saucepan over medium heat and melt the butter.
3. Sauté the garlic and shallot until tender, about 3 minutes.
4. Whisk in the white wine, lemon juice, and orange juice and bring the sauce to a simmer, cooking until it thickens slightly, about 2 minutes.
5. Remove the sauce from the heat and stir in the parsley; set aside.
6. Place a large skillet over medium-high heat and add the olive oil.
7. Panfry the fish until lightly browned and just cooked through, turning them over once, about 10 minutes in total.
8. Serve the fish immediately with a spoonful of sauce for each.

Per serving: Calories 319: Fat 26g: Protein 22g: Carbs 2g

Baked Coconut Haddock

Serves 4 / Prep time: 10 minutes / Cook time: 12 minutes

INGREDIENTS:

4 (5 oz) boneless haddock fillets
Sea salt
Freshly ground pepper

1 cup shredded unsweetened coconut
½ cup ground hazelnuts
2 tbsp coconut oil, melted

DIRECTIONS:

1. Preheat the oven to 400°F. Line a baking sheet with parchment paper and set aside.
2. Pat the fillets dry with paper towels and lightly season the with salt and pepper.
3. Stir together the shredded coconut and hazelnut in a small bowl.
4. Dredge the fish fillets in the coconut mixture so that both sides of each piece are thickly coated.
5. Place the fish on the baking sheet and lightly brush both sides of each piece with the coconut oil.
6. Bake the haddock until the topping is golden and the fish flakes easily with a fork, about 12 minutes total.
7. Serve.

Per serving: Calories 299: Fat 24g: Protein 20g: Carbs 1g

Lemon Butter Chicken

Serves 4 / Prep time: 10 minutes / Cook time: 40 minutes

INSTRUCTIONS:

4 bone-in, skin-on chicken thighs
2 tbsp butter, divided
2 tbsp minced garlic

½ cup Herbed chicken stock
½ cup heavy (whipping) cream
Juice of ½ lemon
Sea salt
Freshly ground black pepper

DIRECTIONS:

1. Preheat oven to 400°F
2. Lightly season the chicken thighs with salt and pepper.
3. Place a large ovenproof skillet over medium-high heat and add 1 tablespoon of butter.
4. Brown the chicken thighs until golden on both sides, about 6 minutes in total. Remove the thighs to a plate and set aside.
5. Add the remaining 1 tablespoon of butter and sauté the garlic until translucent, about 2 minutes.
6. Whisk in the chicken stock, heavy cream and lemon juice
7. Bring the sauce to a boil and then return the chicken to the skillet.
8. Place the skillet in the oven, covered, and braise until the chicken is cooked through, about 30 minutes.

Per serving: Calories 294: Fat 26g: Protein 12 g: Carbs3g

Paprika Chicken

Serves 4 / Prep time: 10 minutes / Cook time: 25 minutes

INGREDIENTS:

4 (4oz) chicken breasts, skin-on
Sea slat
Freshly ground black pepper
1 tbsp olive oil
½ cup chopped sweet onion

½ cup heavy (whipping) cream
2 tsp smoked paprika
½ cup sour cream
2 tbsp chopped fresh parsley

DIRECTIONS:

1. Lightly season the chicken with salt and pepper.
2. Place a large skillet over medium-high heat and add the olive oil.
3. Sear the chicken on both sides until almost cooked through, about 15 minutes in total. Remove the chicken to a plate.
4. Add the onion to the skillet and sauté until tender, about 4 minutes.
5. Stir in the cream and paprika and bring the liquid to a simmer.
6. Return the chicken and any accumulated juices to the skillet and simmer the chicken for 5 minutes until completely cooked.
7. Stir in the sour cream and remove the skillet from the heat
8. Serve topped with the parsley.

Per serving: Calories 389: Fat 30g: Protein 25g: Carbs 4g

STUFFED CHICKEN BREASTS

Serves 4 / Prep time: 60 minutes / Cook time: 30 minutes

INGREDIENTS:

1 tbsp butter

¼ cup chopped sweet onion

½ cup goat cheese, at room temperature

¼ cup Kalamata olives, chopped

¼ cup chopped roasted red pepper

2 tbsp chopped fresh basil

4 (5 oz) chicken breasts, skin-on

2 tbsp extra-virgin olive oil

DIRECTIONS:

1. Preheat the oven to 400°F.
2. In a small skillet over medium heat, melt the butter and add the onion. Sauté until tender, about 3 minutes.
3. Transfer the onion to a medium bowl, and add the cheese, olives, red pepper, and basil. Stir until well blended, then refrigerate for about 30 minutes.
4. Cut horizontal pockets into each chicken breast, and stuff them evenly with the filling. Secure the two sides of each breast with toothpicks.
5. Place a large ovenproof skillet over medium-high heat and add the olive oil.
6. Brown the chicken on both sides, about 10 minutes in total.
7. Place the skillet in the oven and roast until the chicken is just cooked through, about 15 minutes. Remove the toothpicks and serve.

Per serving: Calories 389: Fat 30g: Protein 25g: Carbs 3g

Coconut Chicken

Serves 4 / Prep time: 15 minutes / Cook time: 25 minutes

INGREDIENTS:

2 tablespoons olive oil
4 (4 oz) chicken breasts, cut
into 2-inch chunks
½ cup chopped sweet onion
1 cup coconut milk

1 tablespoon curry powder
1 teaspoon ground cumin
1 teaspoon ground coriander
¼ cup chopped fresh cilantro

DIRECTIONS:

1. Place a large saucepan over medium-high heat and add the olive oil.
2. Sauté the chicken until almost cooked through, about 10 minutes.
3. Add the onion and sauté for an additional 3 minutes.
4. In a medium bowl, whisk together the coconut milk, curry powder cumin, and coriander.
5. Pour the sauce into the saucepan with the chicken and bring the liquid to a boil.
6. Reduce the heat and simmer until the chicken is tender and the sauce has thickened, about 10 minutes.
7. Serve the chicken with the sauce, topped with cilantro.

Per serving: Calories 382: Fat 31g: Protein 23g: Carbs 5g

Buffalo Drumsticks with Chili Aioli

Serves 4 / Prep time: 15 minutes / Cook time: 40 minutes

INGREDIENTS:

2 lbs. chicken drumsticks or
chicken wings
2 tbsp olive oil or coconut oil
2 tbsp white wine vinegar
1 tbsp tomato paste

1 tbsp salt
1 tsp paprika powder
1 tbsp tabasco
Butter or olive oil for greasing
the baking dish

Chili aioli
2/3 cup mayonnaise
1 tbsp smoked paprika powder or
smoked chili powder
1 garlic clove, minced

DIRECTIONS:

1.   Preheat oven to 450°F.
2.   Put the drumsticks in a plastic bag.
3.   Mix the ingredients for the marinade in a small bowl and pour into the plastic bag. Shake the bag thoroughly and let marinate for 10 minutes in room temperature.
4.   Coat a baking dish with oil. Place the drumsticks in the baking dish and let bake for 30-40 minutes or until they are done and have turned a nice color.
5.   Mix together mayonnaise, garlic and chili.
6.   Serve warm

Per Serving: Calories 330: Fat 56g: Protein 42g: Carbs 2g

MEATS

Sirloin with Blue Cheese Compound Butter

Bacon-Wrapped Beef Tenderloin

Italian Beef Burgers

Cheeseburger Casserole

Bacon-Wrapped Meatloaf

Keto Cheesesteak Casserole

Balsamic Roast Beef

Greek Style Lamb Chops

Asian Beef Short Ribs

Buffalo Turkey Meatballs

SIRLOIN WITH BLUE CHEESE COMPOUND BUTTER

Serves 4 / Prep time: 10 minutes, plus 1-hour chill time / Cook time: 12 minutes

INGREDIENTS:

6 tbsp butter, room temperature
4 ounces blue cheese
1 tbsp olive oil

4 (5 ounce) beef sirloin steaks
Sea salt
Freshly ground black pepper

DIRECTIONS:

1. Set the steaks out until they reach room temperature. Set aside.
2. Place the butter in a blender and pulse until the butter is whipped, about 2 minutes.
3. Add the cheese and pulse until just incorporated.
4. Spoon the butter mixture onto a sheet of plastic wrap and roll it into a log about 1 ½ inches in diameter by twisting both ends of the plastic wrap in opposite directions.
5. Refrigerate the butter until completely set, about 1 hour.
6. Slice the butter into ½ inch disks and set them on a plate in the refrigerator until you are ready to serve the steaks. Store leftover butter in the refrigerator for up to 1 week.
7. Rub the steaks all over with the olive oil and season them with salt and pepper.
8. Grill the steaks until they reach your desired doneness, about 6 minutes on each side for medium.
9. Let the steaks rest for 10 minutes. Serve each topped with a disk of the compound butter.

Per serving: Calories 544: Fat 44g: Protein 35g: Carbs 0g:

Bacon-Wrapped Beef Tenderloin

Serves 4 / Prep time: 10 minutes / Cook time: 15 minutes

The full flavor of the bacon wrap combines with the beef tenderloin to create a rich, salty flavor your entire family will enjoy.

INGREDIENTS:

4 (4ounce) beef tenderloin steaks

Freshly ground black pepper

8 bacon slices

1 tbsp extra-virgin olive oil

Sea salt

DIRECTIONS:

1. Preheat the oven to 450°F.
2. Season the steaks with salt and pepper.
3. Wrap each steak snugly around the edges with 2 slices of bacon and secure the bacon with toothpicks.
4. Place a large skillet over medium-high heat and add the olive oil.
5. Pan sear the steaks for 4 minutes per side and transfer them to a baking sheet.
6. Roast the steaks until they reach your desired doneness, about 6 minutes for medium.
7. Remove the steaks from the oven and let them rest for 10 minutes.
8. Remove the toothpicks and serve.

Per serving: Calories 565: Fat 49g: Protein 28g: Carbs 0g

Italian Beef Burgers

Serves 4 / Prep Time: 10 minutes / Cook time: 12 minutes

It's the toppings that make the burger in most cases. You can top these juicy burgers with your favorite items such as bacon, avocado, tomato slices or sliced onion. You can even use all the toppings together to create a Monster Burger!

INGREDIENTS:

1 pound 75% lean ground beef
¼ cup ground almonds
2 tbsp chopped fresh basil
1 tsp minced garlic
¼ tsp sea salt
1 tbsp olive oil
1 tomato cut into 4 thick slices
¼ sweet onion, sliced thinly

DIRECTIONS:

1. In a medium bowl, mix together the ground beef, ground almonds, basil, garlic, and salt until well mixed.
2. Form the beef mixture into four equal patties and flatten them to about ½ inch thick.
3. Place a large skillet on medium-high heat and add the olive oil.
4. Panfry the burgers until cooked through, flipping them once, about 12 minutes in total.
5. Pat away excess grease with a paper towel and serve the burgers with a slice of tomato and onion.

Per serving: Calories 441: Fat 37g: Protein 22g: Carbs 4g

Cheeseburger Casserole

Serves 6 / Prep time: 10 minutes / Cook time: 40 minutes

INGREDIENTS:

1 pound lean ground beef
½ cup chopped sweet onion
2 tsp minced garlic
1 ½ cups shredded aged Cheddar cheese

1 large tomato, chopped
1 tsp minced fresh basil
¼ tsp sea salt
Freshly ground black pepper
½ cup heavy (whipping) cream

DIRECTIONS:

1. Preheat the oven to 350°F.
2. Place a large skillet over medium-high heat and add the ground beef.
3. Brown the beef until cooked through, about 6 minutes, and spoon of any excess fat.
4. Stir in the onion and garlic and cook until the vegetables are tender, about 4 minutes.
5. Transfer the beef and vegetables to an 8-by-8-inch casserole dish.
6. In a medium bowl, stir together 1 cup of shredded cheese and the heavy cream, tomato, basil, salt and pepper until well combined.
7. Pour the cream mixture over the beef mixture and top the casserole with the remaining ½ cup of shredded cheese.
8. Bake until the casserole is bubbly and cheese is melted and lightly browned, about 30 minutes.
9. Serve.

Per serving: Calories 410: Fat 33g: Protein 20g: Carbs 3g

Bacon Wrapped Meatloaf

Serves 4 / Prep time 10 minutes / cook time 1 hour

INGREDIENTS:

2 tbsp butter
1 yellow onion, finely chopped
25 ounces of ground beef
½ cup heavy whipping cream
½ cup shredded cheese
7 ounces sliced bacon

1 egg
1 tbsp dried oregano
1 tsp sea salt
½ tsp black pepper
1 ¼ cups heavy whipping cream (for gravy)
½ tbsp soy sauce

DIRECTIONS:

1. Preheat oven to 400°F.
2. Fry the onion until soft but not browned.
3. Mix the ground beef in a bowl. Add all other ingredients, except the bacon. Mix well, but avoid overworking it.
4. Form into a loaf pan, then wrap with bacon.
5. Bake for approximately 45 minutes. If the bacon begins to overcook before the meat is done, cover with aluminum foil and lower the heat a bit.
6. Save the juices that accumulate in the baking dish and use to make gravy. Mix the juices and heavy cream in a smaller sauce pan.
7. Bring to a boil and lower heat, let simmer for 10 – 15 minutes until it has the right consistency. You can add the soy sauce for extra flavor.
8. Serve with freshly boiled broccoli or cauliflower with butter, salt and pepper.

Per serving: Calories 1038: Fat 90g: Protein 48g: Net carbs 6g

Keto Cheesesteak Casserole

Serves 4 / Prep time 10 minutes / Cook time 20 minutes

INGREDIENTS:

4 oz butter
10 oz mushrooms
1 yellow onion
2 green bell peppers
1 pound ribeye steak, thinly sliced
1 glove garlic
1 tbsp Italian seasoning

1 tsp chili flakes
7 oz shredded provolone cheese
Salt and pepper
4 tbsp unsweetened marinara sauce
½ teaspoon of olive oil for drizzle
Green leafies for topping

DIRECTIONS:

1. Preheat oven to 450°F.
2. Slice or chop mushrooms. Finely chop onion and bell pepper.
3. Fry the vegetables in butter until slightly soft. Put aside.
4. Slice the meat and fry in the same frying pan. Add the garlic and spices. Season with salt and pepper.
5. Return the veggies to the pan and stir.
6. Place everything in a greased baking dish and sprinkle the cheese on top.
7. Bake for 15 – 20 minutes or until the casserole turns golden brown.
8. Drizzle marinara sauce on top and serve with leafy greens and olive oil.

Per serving: Calories 806: Fat 68g: Protein 40g: Carb 9g

Slow Cooker Balsamic Roast Beef

Serves 4 / Prep time 10 minutes / Cook time 8 hours

INGREDIENTS:

1 ¾ pound boneless round roast

1 cup beef broth

1 tbsp stevia

1 tbsp soy sauce

1 tbsp Worcestershire sauce

4 cloves garlic, chopped

¼ tsp red pepper flakes

DIRECTIONS:

1. Place the roast beef in the slow cooker.
2. In a mixing bowl, mix all other ingredients and pour over the roast.
3. Let it sit in the slow cooker for six to eight hours.
4. Once cooked, remove from the slow cooker and break the meat apart.
5. You can add a dollop of sour cream and chopped scallions to top off each serving.

Per serving: Calories 355: Protein 59g: Fat 9.7g: Carbohydrates 8g

GREEK STYLE LAMB CHOPS

Servings: 4 / Prep time 10 minutes / Cook time 6 minutes

INGREDIENTS:

1 tbsp black pepper	2 tsp olive oil
1 tbsp dried oregano	2 tsp seal salt
1 tbsp minced garlic	8 pieces of lamb loin chops,
2 tbsp lemon juice	around 4 ounces

DIRECTIONS:

1. In a big bowl or dish, combine the black pepper, salt, minced garlic, lemon juice and oregano. Then rub it equally on all sides of the lamb chops.
2. Then place a skillet on high heat. After a minute, coat skillet with the cooking spray and place the lamb chops in the skillet. Sear chops for a minute on each side.
3. Lower heat to medium, continue cooking chops for 2 -3 minutes per side until desired doneness is reached.
4. Let the chops rest for five minutes before serving.

Per Serving: Calories 457: Protein 63g: Fat 9g: Carbs 4g

Asian Beef Short Ribs

Serves 4 / Prep time: 15 minutes / Cook time: 12 hours

INGREDIENTS:

2 Pounds beef short ribs
1 cup water
1 onion, sliced
1 tbsp Szechuan peppercorns
2 tbsp curry powder

3 tbsp coconut amino
6 pieces star anise
6 tbsp sesame oil
Salt and pepper to taste

DIRECTIONS:

1. Place all ingredients except for the sesame oil in the instant pot.
2. Close the lid and make sure that the steam release valve is set to "Venting".
3. Press the "slow cook" button and adjust the cooking time to 12 hours.
4. Once cooked, remove from pot and place into serving dishes. Drizzle with sesame oil, serve.

Per serving: Calories 592: Protein 47 g: Fat 44g: Carbs 6g

Buffalo Turkey Balls

Serves 5 / Prep time: 10 minutes / Cook time: 40 minutes

INGREDIENTS:

2 eggs
1 pound ground turkey
½ cup hot sauce
½ stick unsalted butter

¼ cup almond flour
3 tbsp blue cheese, crumbled
2 oz whipped cream cheese

DIRECTIONS:

1. Preheat oven to 350°F.
2. Mix the turkey meat, cream cheese, egg, blue cheese and almond flour in a mixing bowl. Mix well and evenly divide into 20 small meat balls.
3. Place the meat balls on a greased baking pan.
4. Bake for 15 minutes.
5. While the meatballs are cooking, make the sauce by mixing the butter and hot sauce in a small sauce pan.
6. Remove the meat balls from the oven and dip them in the hot sauce.
7. Place the meatballs in the oven and re-bake for another 15 minutes.
8. Remove the meatballs from the oven and place into serving dishes. Garnish with chopped scallions or parsley.

Per serving: Calories 300: Protein 30g: Fat 18g: Carbs 2g

VEGETABLES

Zucchini Salad

Loaded Baked Cauliflower

Spinach Salad with Hot Bacon Dressing

Coleslaw

Baked Artichokes

Creamy Lemon Green Beans

Thai Curry Cabbage

Low Carb Broccoli Mash

Baked Mini Bell Peppers

Low Carb Onion Rings

Zucchini Salad

Serves 6 / Prep time: 10 minutes / Cook time: 10 minutes

INGREDIENTS:

2 pounds zucchini
2 tbsp butter or olive oil
3 oz celery stalks, finely sliced
2 oz chopped scallions
1 cup mayonnaise

2 tbsp fresh chives, finely chopped
½ tablespoons Dijon Mustard
Sea Salt
Pepper

DIRECTIONS:

1. Peel and cut the zucchini into pieces that are about half an inch thick. Use a spoon to remove the seeds. Place in a colander and add salt. Leave for 5 – 10 minutes and then cautiously press out the water.
2. Fry the cubes in butter for a couple of minutes over medium heat. They should not brown, just slightly soften. Set aside to cool.
3. Mix the other ingredients in a large bowl and add the zucchini once it's cool.

Tip: You can prepare the salad 1-2 days ahead of time; the flavors only enhance with time. You can also add a chopped hard- boiled egg.

Per serving: Calories 312: Protein 3g: Fat 32g: Carbs 4g

Loaded Baked Cauliflower

Servings 2 / Prep time: 10 minutes / Cook time: 30 minutes

INGREDIENTS:

4 ounces bacon
1 pound cauliflower
2/3 cup sour cream
½ pound cheddar cheese, shredded

2 tbsp chives, finely chopped
1 tsp garlic powder
Sea salt
Freshly ground pepper

DIRECTIONS:

1. Preheat oven to 350°F.
2. Chop the bacon into small pieces. Fry until crispy in a hot frying pan. Reserve the fat for serving.
3. Break the cauliflower into florets. Boil until soft in lightly salted water. Drain completely.
4. Chop the cauliflower roughly. Add sour cream and garlic powder. Combine well with ¾ of the cheese and most of the finely chopped chives. Salt and pepper
5. Place in a baking dish and top with the rest of the cheese. Bake in the oven for 10 – 15 minutes or until the cheese has melted.
6. Top with the bacon, the rest of the chives and the bacon fat. Enjoy.

Per serving: Calories 1014: Protein 40g: Fat 89g: Carbs 13g

Spinach Salad with Hot Bacon Dressing

Serves 4 / Prep time: 10 minutes   Cook time: 30 minutes

INGREDIENTS:

Salad:
6 cups fresh spinach
2 hard-boiled eggs, chopped
2 ounce chopped bacon
1/3 cup parmesan cheese,
finely grated

Hot Bacon Fat Dressing:
½ cup bacon fat or light olive
oil
¼ cup apple cider vinegar
1 tbsp Dijon mustard
Sea salt
Freshly ground black pepper

DIRECTIONS:

1. Wash the spinach and remove tough ends. Dry the leaves. Divide the spinach evenly among four salad plates.
2. Top with hard-boiled eggs and bacon divided evenly among the plates. Sprinkle Parmesan cheese on top if desired.
3. Use a small saucepan to heat the bacon fat. Whisk in the apple cider vinegar and remaining ingredients. Serve warm and mix just before pouring.
4. Dress salad plates with hot bacon fat vinaigrette and serve immediately.

Per serving: Calories 344: Protein 6g: Fat 35g: Carbs 1g

Coleslaw

Servings: 4 / Prep time: 5 minutes / Cook time: 5 minutes

INGREDIENTS:

15 ounces green cabbage
1 cup mayonnaise

½ tsp sea salt
¼ tsp freshly ground black pepper

DIRECTIONS:

1. Shred the cabbage with a sharp knife, mandolin slicer or a food processor.
2. Place in a bowl and add mayonnaise, salt and pepper. Stir well and let sit for ten minutes.

Per Serving: Calories 409: Protein 2g: Fat 42g: Carbs 4g

Baked Artichokes

Serves 10 / Pre time: 10 minutes / Cook time: 10 minutes

INGREDIENTS:

10 small fresh artichokes, preferably young
4 tbsp olive oil (use half for cooking, the other half for baking)

1 teaspoon Sea Salt
Freshly ground black pepper
Additional salt for taste

DIRECTIONS:

1. Preheat the oven to 350°F.
2. Place the artichokes on a sturdy work surface. Take the artichoke stem in one hand and cut off the top half of the artichoke.
3. If it's there, scrap out the fuzzy choke at the center of the leaves with a small spoon.
4. Turn the artichoke around and cut the stem off. Remove the hard leaves at the bottom until only soft leaves remain.
5. Place the artichokes in a pot and add enough water to cover. Add a little olive oil and season with salt and pepper.
6. Bring to a boil. Cook for 15 – to 20 minutes, until a leaf can be easily pulled out.
7. Drain the artichokes and place them upright in a baking dish.
8. Drizzle with olive oil and season with salt and pepper.
9. Bake for about 15 minutes until the bottoms of the artichokes are fork-tender, then serve.

Tip: Young artichokes don't usually have a choke yet, which makes them easier to handle.

Per serving: Calories 108: Protein 4g: Fat 6g: Carbs 7g

Creamy Lemon Green Beans

Serves 4 / Prep time: 10 minutes / Cook time: 15 minutes

INGREDIENTS:

10 ounces fresh green beans
3 ounces butter or olive oil
½ tsp sea salt
¼ tsp freshly ground black pepper

1 Cup heavy whipping cream
½ lemon, the zest
½ cup fresh parsley (optional)

DIRECTIONS:

1. Trim and rinse the green beans.
2. Heat butter or oil in a frying pan.
3. Sauté the beans for 3-4 minutes over medium-high heat until they begin to brown. Lower the heat towards the end. Salt and pepper to taste.
4. Add heavy cream and let simmer for 1-2 minutes. Grate the lemon zest finely and sprinkle on top of the green beans before serving.
5. Add finely chopped parsley before serving.

Per serving: Calories 391: Protein 3g: Fat 40g: Carbs 5g

Thai Curry Cabbage

Serves 4 / Prep time: 10 minutes / Cook time: 20 minutes

INGREDIENTS:

3 tbsp coconut oil

1 tbsp red curry paste

30 ounces shredded green cabbage

1 tsp sea salt

1 tbsp sesame oil

DIRECTIONS:

1. Heat up coconut oil in a frying pan or a wok over high heat. Add curry paste and stir for a minute. Add cabbage.
2. Sauté until the cabbage begins to turn golden brown, but still is a little chewy. Stir thoroughly and lower the heat towards the end.
3. Salt to taste. Add sesame oil and sauté for another 1-2 minutes and serve.

Per serving: Calories 181: Protein 3g: Fat 14g: Carbs 8g

Low Carb Broccoli Mash

Serves 4 / Prep time: 10 minutes / Cook time: 5 min

INGREDIENTS:

25 ounces of broccoli

4 tbsp fresh basil or fresh parsley, finely chopped

3 ounces butter

1 garlic clove

Sea salt

Freshly ground black pepper

DIRECTIONS:

1. Chop the broccoli into florets, peel and cut the stem into small pieces.
2. Put approximately 6 cups of water into a large saucepan, lightly salt the water.
3. Boil the broccoli for just a few minutes, just enough to retain a slightly firm texture.
4. Discard the water.
5. Blend with other ingredients in a food processor or use an immersion blender.
6. Salt and pepper to taste. You can add more olive oil or butter if desired.
7. Serve hot.

Per serving: Calories 212: Protein 5g: Fat 18g: Carbs 7g

Baked Mini Bell Peppers

Servings 4 / Prep time: 15 minutes / Cook time: 15 minutes

INGREDIENTS:

8 ounces mini bell peppers, about 2 per serving
1 ounce air-dried chorizo, thinly sliced
1 tbsp fresh thyme or fresh cilantro

1 tbsp mild chipotle paste
2 tbsp olive oil
1 cup shredded cheese
8 ounces cream cheese

DIRECTIONS:

1. Preheat oven to 400°F.
2. Split the bell peppers lengthwise and remove the core.
3. Chop the chorizo and the herbs finely.
4. Mix together cheese, spices and oil in a small bowl. Add the chorizo and herbs. Stir until smooth.
5. Add the mixture to the bell peppers and place in a greased baking dish.
6. Sprinkle shredded cheese on top. Bake in the oven for 15 – 20 minutes or until the cheese is melted and golden brown.

Per serving: Calories 410: Protein 12g: Fat 37g: Carbs 6g

Low Carb Onion Rings

Serves 4 / Prep time: 5 minutes / Cook time: 20 minutes

INGREDIENTS:

1 jumbo onion	½ tsp garlic powder
1 egg	1 pinch sea salt
1 cup almond flour	1 tbsp olive oil
½ cup grated parmesan cheese	1 tbsp garlic powder

DIRECTIONS:

1. Preheat the oven to 400°F, or, turn on the broiler.
2. Peel the onion and slice into rings, about 1 inch thick.
3. Mix the dry ingredients in a bowl. Whisk the egg in another bowl.
4. Dip the onion rings in the egg batter and then in the flour mix, one at a time.
5. Place the rings on a baking sheet covered with parchment paper.
6. Drizzle or spray oil on the rings and bake in the oven for 15 – 20 minutes. If you are using the broiler, keep a close eye on them: they are done when golden brown and crisp.

Per serving: Calories 323: Protein 15g: Fat 26g: Carbs 5g

DESSERTS

Chocolate Mug Muffin

Low Carb Chocolate Mousse

Strawberry Cheesecake Fat Bombs

Chocolate Chip Cookie Dough Fat Bomb

Keto Tiramisu

No Bake Keto Mocha Cheesecake

Cream Cheese Cookies

Avocado Brownies

Avocado Frozen Yogurt

Blueberry Mug Cake

Chocolate Mug Muffin

Serves 2 / Prep time: 2 minutes / Cook time: 2 minutes

INGREDIENTS:

2 tbsp almond four
1 tbsp cocoa powder
1 tbsp Swerve
½ tsp baking powder
¼ tsp vanilla extract
1 egg

1 pinch sea salt
1 ½ tbsp melted coconut oil or butter
½ ounce sugar-free dark chocolate
½ tsp coconut oil or butter for greasing the mugs

DIRECTIONS:

1. Combine dry ingredients in a small bowl. Stir in egg and melted coconut oil or butter. Mix until smooth.
2. Add coarsely chopped chocolate and pour into two well-greased coffee mugs.
3. Microwave for 90 seconds. Remove and let cool
4. Serve with a dollop of whipped coconut cream.

Per serving: Calories 230: Protein 6g: Fat 21g: Carbs 2g

Low Carb Chocolate Mousse

Serves 6/ Prep time: 2 hour / Cook time: 15 minutes

INGREDIENTS:

1 ¼ cups heavy whipping
cream
½ tsp vanilla extract
2 egg yolks

1 pinch sea salt
3 ounces dark chocolate with a
minimum of 80% cocoa solids

DIRECTIONS:

1. Break or chop the chocolate into small pieces. Melt in the microwave (20 second intervals, stirring in between). Set aside at room temperature to cool.
2. Whip the cream to soft peaks. Add vanilla towards the end.
3. Mix egg yolks with salt in a separate bowl.
4. Add the melted chocolate to the egg yolks and mix to a smooth batter.
5. Add a couple of spoonsful of whipped cream to the chocolate mix and stir to loosen it a bit. Add the remaining cream and fold it through.
6. Divide the batter into ramekins or serving glasses of your choice. Place in the fridge and let chill for at least 2 hours. Serve as is, or top with fresh berries.

Per serving: Calories 270: Protein 3g: Fat 25g: Carbs 6g

Strawberry Cheesecake Fat Bombs

Servings 14 / Prep time: 10 minutes / Total time: 10 minutes

INGREDIENTS:

½ cup strawberries
¾ cup cream cheese, softened
¼ cup butter

2 tbsp powdered erythritol
½ teaspoon vanilla extract

DIRECTIONS:

1. Place the cream cheese and butter (cut into small pieces) into a mixing bowl. Leave at room temperature for 30 - 60 minutes.
2. Meanwhile, wash the strawberries and remove the green parts. Place the in a bowl and mash, using a fork or place in a blender for a smooth texture.
3. Add the powdered erythritol, vanilla extract and mix well. Before you mix the strawberries with the remaining ingredients, make sure they have reached room temperature.
4. Add to the bowl with the softened butter and cream cheese.
5. Use a hand whisk or food processor and mix until well combined.
6. Spoon the mixture into small muffin silicon molds, or candy molds. Place in the freezer for about 2 hours or until set.
7. When done, unmold the fat bombs and place into a container. Keep in the freezer and enjoy any time.

Per serving: Calories 67: Protein 0.96g: Fat 7.4g: Carbs 0.85g

Chocolate Chip Cookie Dough Fat Bombs

INGREDIENTS:

8 ounces cream cheese, softened
1 stick (1/2 cup) salted butter
½ cup creamy peanut butter or almond butter
1/3 cup swerve sweetener

1 tsp vanilla extract
4 ounces Stevia sweetened chocolate chips (or, unsweetened chocolate chips depending on your taste)

DIRECTIONS:

1. Cream everything together in a mixer and then spray a cookie scoop with coconut oil cooking spray.
2. Refrigerate dough for 30 minutes before scooping onto parchment paper, then freeze for 30 minutes.
3. Store in refrigerator.

Per serving: Calories 139: Protein 2g: Fat 14g: Carbs 2g

Keto Tiramisu

Serves 4 / Prep time: 10 minutes / Cook time: 2 minutes

INGREDIENTS:

FOR FILLING	FOR MUG CAKE	COFFEE LIQUOR MIX
½ block of cream cheese (at room temperature)	3 tbsp almond flour	1 shot expresso
¾ cup heavy whipping cream	2 tbsp erythritol	1 shot rum
2 -3 tbsp erythritol	1 egg	
	½ tsp baking powder	Cocoa powder to garnish
	1 tsp vanilla extract	

DIRECTIONS:

1. Start by making your coffee mixture. Mix your espresso and rum together and place in the fridge for the mixture to get cold.
2. Make Mug cake. Mix all ingredients together in a mug and microwave on high for 60 seconds. Remove cake from the mug and let it cool for 5 minutes.
3. Slice the cake into four equal pieces and place them on a cooling rack to let them completely cool down.
4. For the cream: In a bowl, combine cream cheese, vanilla extract and erythritol. Using an electric hand mixer, combine all ingredients until sweetener has completely dissolved and texture is very smooth.
5. In a separate bowl, pour heavy whipping cream and whisk on high speed until medium to stiff peaks form, about 1 minute. Do not over beat.
6. Add whipped cream into the cream cheese mixture and whisk on low speed until the cream cheese is well

incorporated into the cream. This should take 45 seconds to 1 minute.

7. Take your coffee mixture out of the fridge and dip your sliced almond cake into it. Make sure your cake is completely soaked. Now place one cake slice on the bottom of the cup/mug you will be serving in, and scoop in 2 tablespoons of the cream filling.

8. Repeat this step one more time to finish building up your tiramisu cup.

9. Drizzle some unsweetened cocoa powder on top of your dessert. Repeat for each serving.

10. For best results, refrigerate for 2 hours before serving.

Per serving: Calories 314: Protein 5g: Fat 29g: Carbs 11.9g: Fiber7.2g

No Bake Keto Mocha Cheesecake

Serves 4 / Prep time: 10 minutes / Total time: 10 minutes

INGREDIENTS:

¾ cup heavy whipping cream
1 block of cream cheese (room temperature)
¼ cup unsweetened cocoa

¾ cup Swerve Confectioners sweetener
1 double shot of espresso

DIRECTIONS:

1. Place the softened cream cheese in a bowl, and using a hand mixer, whip the cream cheese for 1 minute. Add espresso and continue mixing.
2. Add the sweetener, ¼ cup at a time and mix. Be sure to taste periodically, you may not need to use all the sweetener.
3. Add cocoa powder and mix until completely blended.
4. In a separate bowl, whip the cream until stiff peaks form.
5. Gently fold the whipped cream into the mocha mixture using a spatula.
6. Place in individual serving dishes. Enjoy!

Per serving: Calories 425: Protein 6g: Fat 33g: Carbs 3.6g

Keto Cream Cheese Cookies

Servings: 24 / Prep Time: 10 minutes / Cook time: 10 minutes

INGREDIENTS:

¼ cup butter (softened)
2 ounces plain cream cheese (softened)
½ cup erythritol
2 tsp vanilla extract
3 cups almond flour
¼ tsp sea salt
1 large egg white

DIRECTIONS:

1. Preheat oven to 350°F. Line a large cookie sheet with parchment paper.
2. Use a hand mixer to beat together the butter, cream cheese, and erythritol: beat until fluffy and light in color.
3. Beat in the vanilla extract, salt and egg white.
4. Beat in almond flour, ½ cup at a time.
5. Use a medium cookie scoop to scoop balls of dough onto the prepared cookie sheet. Flatten with your palm.
6. Bake for 15 minutes, until the edges are lightly golden. Allow to cool completely in the pan before handling (cookies will harden as they cool).

Serving size: 2 cookies.

Per serving: Calories 106: Protein 3g: Fat 9g: Carbs 3g

Keto Avocado Brownies

Servings: 10 /Prep time:10 minutes/Cook time: 25 minutes

INGREDIENTS:

½ cup avocado, mashed
½ cup almond butter
3 tbsp artificial sweetener
2 tbsp cocoa powder

1 tbsp olive oil
1 tsp vanilla extract
½ cup dark chocolate baking chips
¼ cup chopped pecans (optional)

DIRECTIONS:

1. Preheat oven to 350°F.
2. Mash 1 to 1 ½ avocados until you have ½ cup of well mashed avocado.
3. Using a medium sized mixing bowl, add the mashed avocado and almond butter, beat on high for 2 minutes or until the mixture is creamy and smooth.
4. Mix in sweetener and cocoa powder. Blend until ingredients are well combined.
5. Add olive oil and vanilla extract. Stir well until mixture is smooth.
6. Fold in baking chips and chopped pecans.
7. Spread the mixture into a well-greased 8x8 baking pan.
8. Bake for 20 – 25 minutes. Let the brownies cool for at least 10 minutes before you serve.

Per serving: Calories 680: Protein 9g: Fat 13g: Carbs 7g

Low Carb Butter Cookies

Prep time: 10 minutes / Cook time: 10 minutes

INGREDIENTS:

1 cup almond flour
¼ cup Confectioners Swerve

3 tbsp salted butter (room temperature)
½ tsp vanilla extract

DIRECTIONS:

1. Preheat oven to 350°F.
2. Prepare a baking sheet lined with parchment paper or a nonstick baking mat.
3. In a mixing bowl, combine all ingredients, stirring thoroughly until resembling a dough. (it will look crumbly while you stir, then will form into a cohesive dough)
4. Form 1-inch balls, placing them on the baking sheet. There should be about 12 balls, separated from each other by about 2 inches.
5. Flatten each dough ball using a fork, then rotate 90 degrees and flatten again, forming a crisscross pattern.
6. Bake at 350°F until the cookie are golden around the edges, 8-10 minutes depending on the thickness of the cookies.
7. Let cool completely before removing them from the baking sheet, they cookies will be very soft when they first come out of the oven.

Per serving: Calories 80: Protein 2g: Fat 8g: Carbs 1.5g

Avocado Frozen Yogurt

Serves 4 / Prep time: 10 minutes / Cook time 10 minutes

INGREDIENTS:

2 ½ cups whipping cream (sugar-free)
1 cup Greek yogurt
1 tbsp cherry extract (sugar-free)

1 tsp Stevia powder
1 tbsp arrowroot powder
½ avocado, cut into chunks
1 ounce gelatin

DIRECTIONS:

1. In a large mixing bowl combine Greek yogurt, cherry extract, stevia and arrowroot powder and 2 cups whipping cream. With an electric mixer, blend for 2-3 minutes on high speed. Pour the mixture into serving glasses and place in freezer for 30-40 minutes.
2. Boil the gelatin with a cup of water. Stir well to dissolve the gelatin completely. When done, remove from the heat and allow the gelatin to cool to room temperature.
3. Chop the avocado into bite-sized pieces after slicing them in half and peeling off the skin. Set aside.
4. Add 2 tablespoons of gelatin on top of the frozen yogurt. Put some avocado chunks as well. Put in the rest of the whipping cream and replace in the freezer for another 15 minutes.
5. Serve cold.

Per serving: Calories 285: Protein 13g: Fat24g: Carbs 4.9g

BLUEBERRY MUG CAKE

Serves 2 / Prep time: 3 minutes / Cook time: 2 minutes

INGREDIENTS:

2 tbsp coconut flour	2 tbsp cream cheese
½ tsp baking powder	1 tbsp butter
25 grams fresh blueberries	15 – 20 drips Liquid Stevia
1 large egg	¼ tsp Himalayan Salt

DIRECTONS:

1. Add the butter and cream cheese to a mug and microwave for 20 seconds. Mix with a fork.
2. Add the baking powder, coconut flour and stevia and combine with a fork.
3. Add the egg and combine.
4. Add the salt and fresh blueberries, and fold gently.
5. Microwave for 90 seconds.
6. Eat right out of the mug, or flip out onto a plate. For added flavor dust with powdered swerve.

Per serving: Calories 345: Protein 10g: Fat 29g: Carbs 13g

Our Keto Diet is all about the fat. And since this eating plan requires up to 80% of our caloric intake to be from a fat source, it's definitely going to be the nutrient we focus on most. Although our diet requires it, we have to make healthier choices – not just any old fat will do. Our main objective is to consume enough healthy fats, while at the same time avoiding those fat sources that are less than optimum choices. Some people try to simplify the keto diet by thinking that they just need to eat a lot of fat and avoid carbs, but you can very quickly eat an excessive amount of unhealthy fat if you maintain that mind set.

Resources on choosing fats is scare. For so many years we were told adamantly to avoid all fats because they caused too many health issues. What we do know is that sources of unsaturated fat are still the recommendation over saturated fats, even though both are keto-friendly. Proven to be anti-inflammatory and heart-healthy, these unsaturated fats are the best, healthiest choice.

You can eat higher-fat protein foods, like bacon and sausage, but it's easier to control the amounts of fat you consume if you choose instead to use those fats you simply add into your foods. Bacon and sausage have a lot of calories, protein, and saturated fat. It's much easier to continue the keto way of eating once your hit your goal weight by simply omitting the added fats. Once you hit your goal weight, if you continue to eat the high-fat foods like bacon and sausage, the likelier you are to regain the weight.

Just keep in mind that while pure sources of fat, such as olive oil and coconut oil contain zero carbs, other sources like nut butter or avocado (although they may be primarily fat) also have carbohydrates that need to be counted in your daily totals.

Your individual caloric needs and goals will specify how much you eat while on the keto diet, but as on any diet overconsumption of fat can cause weight gain. It is important to spread out your fats evenly throughout the day.

BEST SOURCES OF FAT

The best fats that you can eat plenty of on the keto diet are:

- Avocado: a rich source of heart-healthy monounsaturated fatty acids (MUFAs). They are also packed with fiber to bolster digestive health. One-half of an avocado contains 161 calories, 2 grams of protein, 15 grams of fat, 9 grams of total carbs, and 7 grams of fiber (bringing it to 2 grams of net carbs)
- Olive oil: Olive oil is great for light sautéing, using in dressings, or drizzling over cooked meats or vegetables as a finishing oil. One tablespoon offers 119 calories and 13.5 grams of fat, only 2 grams of which are saturated fat (according to the USDA)
- Avocado Oil: Avocado oil is rich in anti-inflammatory MUFAs, and best of all, it stands up to high-heat cooking. The average smoke point for avocado oil is

500°F. Again, according to the USDA, 1 tablespoon of avocado oil has 124 calories, 14 grams of fat, and 0 grams of carbohydrates.

- Nuts and Nut Butter: Although nuts offer unsaturated fats, they also contain carbs, so look at the labels to calculate exactly what you're getting. For example, 1 tablespoon of almond butter has 98 calories, 3 grams of protein, 9 grams of fat, 3 grams of total carbs and about 1.5 grams of fiber. Another good thing to note, is that 1-ounce serving of almonds (approximately 23 almonds) has 164 calories, 6 grams of protein, 14 grams of fat, 6 grams of carbohydrates, and 3.5 grams of fiber.

- Chia Seeds and Flaxseed: These keto diet staples are rich with omega 3 fatty acids. It is suggested that while on the keto diet you try to get more of these fats in order to improve the ratio of omega-6s to 3s which some research suggests, optimized health. 1 ounce of chia seeds has 138 calories, 5 grams of protein, 9 grams of fat, 12 grams of carbs, and a whopping 10 grams of fiber (which means only 2 grams of net carbs!).

  1 tablespoon of flaxseed has 37 calories, 1 gram of protein, 3grams of fat, 2 grams of carbs, and 2 grams of fiber (which means, basically, 0 net carbs!). Just be sure to buy ground flaxseed so your body can absorb their omega 3s.

NOT ALL FATS ARE CREATED EQUAL

While many recipes call for cheeses, cream, butter, and coconut oil, these are four types of fat which should be limited.

- Cheese: a slice of cheese contains 115 calories, 7 grams of protein, 9 grams of fat, (5 grams of saturated fat), about ½ gram of carbohydrate, and no fiber. The saturated fat qualifies it as a food you should limit, but some research suggests the food has health benefits as well. A study published in December of 2017 found that cheese eating was associated with a 10 percent lower risk of heart disease and stroke, particularly for those consuming about 1.5 ounces (or a slice and a half) per day.
- Cream: Adding heavy cream or half-and-half to your coffee is one way to get additional source of fat into your day (which helped to create the Bulletproof Coffee everyone is crazy about!). Just realize that it is a source of saturated fat – and given the small serving size, it's easy to go overboard. 1 tablespoon has 51 calories, 5 grams of fat (3.5 grams of saturated fat) and is just shy of ½ gram of carbohydrate.
- Butter: It's been stated that eating a significant amount of butter has some of the worst effects on your health compared with other fats. It is okay to use butter in your fat rotation, but best not to make it your go-to fat source. Instead opt for more unsaturated sources. 1 tablespoon of butter has 102 calories, 12 grams of fat (7 grams are saturated fat) and 0 carbs.
- Coconut Oil: Given that coconut oil is trendy, it's been credited as a panacea for health ills; and given the

general go-ahead to consume as much as you want. That's not exactly the case. Because of its high levels of saturated fats (which are the ones that clog arteries), there is still a level of controversy over its inclusion as a safe fat. The argument some make is that coconut oil is different. Part of its fat is made up of medium-chain triglycerides, fatty acids that the body metabolizes quicker and are less likely to get stored by the body as fat. The USDA indicates that 1 tablespoon has 121 calories, 13 grams of fat (11 of which are saturated fats), and 0 carbohydrates. Eat the healthier unsaturated sources of fat first, then moderate amounts of these saturated sources.

All of which brings us to the one fat you must stay away from, keto diet or not.

FATS TO BE AVOIDED

- Trans Fat: Everyone should stay away from consuming added trans fats. While these are naturally found in some meat and milk, they're often added to processed foods. This is just another great reason to stay as far away from processed foods as possible; while you're on the keto diet, and when you're not. Processed foods are a whole other topic!

It's not as difficult as it sounds to choose the right fat sources to compliment your new keto-way-of-eating. Choose mainly from the first list and you can't go wrong. Use the fat sources from the second group in moderation, and simply avoid any processed foods at this point. It will only increase your likelihood of success if you do some research on your own regarding processed foods. For now, its best to avoid them.

Fats are THE most important nutrient of the diet. You should familiarize yourself with the different types of fats and do more extensive research in an effort to become an expert. Next to finding and understanding your macro needs, this is probably the best single thing you can do to ensure your success on this keto diet.

There are multiple sources of information on the internet. You can find macro calculators, recipes, resources and help simply by googling "keto." The plethora of keto information can be overwhelming at first, but if you stick to it you will learn so much that you'll wonder how you ever lived without keto before!

God has created a beautifully complex human body; and left us in charge of taking care of it. The more you learn, the better you will be able to do just this. Many health issues can be eliminated or improved by following the keto diet. The more you research, the more you learn, the better you will be able to fulfill your Calling. Obedience is a key element in building and continuing your personal relationship with the Lord.

Casting down imaginations, and every high thing that exalteth itself against the knowledge of God, and bringing into captivity every thought to the obedience of Christ.   2 Corinthians 10:5

I pray that you have found this book helpful, not only in beginning your path to good health, but also in helping you to rekindle your desire to learn more about God. Growing as a Christian is our ultimate goal, and I hope you find this book helpful on your journey.

Implement strategies to prevent temptation. Pray before you enter any restaurant, or step into the restroom before you order and take a few minutes to get your soul and mind ready. There is no greater choice to make, then that of keeping God in all things, as part of everything in your life. This includes changing, growing, and creating new eating habits. Prayers at this point will not only help you to stay strong in you resolve, but will bring you a renewed sense of peace that will last for hours. Because once you pray, you *will* make the right choices.

Become a Rock.

Matthew 16:18

And I tell you, you are Peter, and on this rock I will build my church, and the gates of hell shall not prevail against it.

You are creating and maintaining a Holy Temple of God. It is to be provided an environment where it can thrive. It should be nourished properly and protected at all cost.

EPILOGUE

Life in itself is a challenge. When faced with the added trials that come from having a damaging obsession with food, all too often our spiritual life will suffer. Every good therapist (and lay person for that matter) will tell you that admitting the problem is the first step to overcoming it. If you are suffering from a food addiction, or have developed a lifetime of poor eating habits, then you have likely made the decision to overlook God's Word on gluttony. It is an easy thing to do in this society that has strayed so far from God's original plan. Multi-cultural societal stress, high divorce rates, economic stress, faltering family stability and so much more have all added to what many have come to believe is the need to manipulate God's Word, the Holy Bible, and make it work for *us*, instead of us working to follow it's outline for our lives. This is no fault of yours: I do not mean to tell you that you are or have been a bad Christian. You have either been directly lied to, or led down a path that was founded on deceit which has been years in the making. You were, more or less, born into it. It is not your fault.

We have become a society that picks and chooses those parts of God's Word that work for us and to simply omit those that may interfere with our lifestyles. Overeating, or gluttony, is one of those sins that society has arbitrarily determined we can delete from our *Rules to Living a Christian Life*. The Bible however, repeatedly tells us this is not the case. The Bible tells us that overeating will lead to damnation.

Philippians 3:19 says "Their end is destruction, their god is their belly, and they glory in their shame, with minds set on earthly things".

Yet, over the years our society has continued to put their physical desires above scripture, and continue to harvest only those scriptures that work for them. The practice of "Picking and Choosing" scripture is not in your best interest either spiritually or physically. It is simply another way Satan has found to undermine God's Word in our everyday lives.

We are living in an age of deceit. It is everywhere. Deceit has almost become a thing to be proud of. It is the Fake News, it is glorified in movies, television shows, and used limitlessly on the internet. Affecting the Christian most are those people who develop their own doctrine, adhering to their own belief systems and calling it religion. You name a belief, and it's out there somewhere with a large following and plenty of scripture to back it up. This is the age of False Prophets; and Facebook, YouTube, and even local churches have provided the platforms for them to flourish. The internet allows preachers of all types to teach any kind of doctrine they choose without restraint. Unfortunately, gullible Christians anywhere in the world will watch, and listen, and be deceived. A preacher using scriptures out of context to back up false doctrine is an especially difficult thing to perceive, and leads to a treacherous path.

Many Christian denominations have fast-tracked their way to damnation by formulating their own doctrines and picking and choosing verses that support those doctrines while ignoring others that might discredit them. Many Christians have been led astray by these churches and their false doctrines and have lived their lives unwittingly following liars and charlatans.

You can think of it as a type of buffet, or "designer" religion; instead of taking in the wholeness of the Word, these false prophets reach in and take those verses that seem to support their views, those that do not "cramp their style," and custom fit them to create their own unique religious experience. By omitting the surrounding scripture, or interpreting it in such a way as to make it comprehendible, the true message is taken out of context and delivers a completely different message. For many, it makes them feel more "comfortable" to follow these designer religions because it creates a false sense of security by feeding into their own failures and justifying their sinful natures.

Our beliefs have become compromised because of it. Cherry-Picking scriptures is a reckless practice that believers and non-believers alike can fall prey to. Regardless of the reasons behind this practice, whether it is to prove that their beliefs are right and others are wrong, or to try and justify specific sinful behaviors, this practice will destroy any current spiritual relationship with God and ensure the inability to develop one.

Gluttony is a sin. Pure, and simple. That is a fact. It is written in God's Holy Word and cannot be disputed. You can't pick and choose your way out of this one.

So, whether you eat or drink, or whatever you do, do all to the glory of God. 1 Corinthians 10:31

We must take God at His Word, his full Word, and strive to fully understand the scriptures in their entirety. When we decide to ignore scriptures that we either disagree with, or don't fully understand, we put a wedge between ourselves and our Creator.

Shall mortal man be more just than God? shall a man be more pure than his maker?

Job 4:17 asks us to look closely at our own motives, and to question our desire to put ourselves into God's place by either rewriting His scripture, or ignoring it.

We have been forewarned of the coming of false prophets, and harbingers of evil.

1 Timothy 4:1: Now the Spirit speaketh expressly, that in the latter times some shall depart from the faith, giving heed to seducing spirits, and doctrines of devils.

It is our responsibility to listen, but also to question those that bring us the Word of God. We must pray for a discerning spirit that will allow us to know when scripture has been omitted, or taken out of context by deceitful means.

Few sermons are given on the sin of gluttony. It is an uncomfortable topic, because it is a sin that many ministers themselves have succumbed to. Obesity has become an epidemic; one that the church is not speaking much about. You won't hear sermons on it, or see any study guides for your Sunday School class to discuss. Yet these things should be provided. We have to stop ignoring the issue, and learn to help people who are struggling with the debilitating consequences of overeating. We as individuals must heed God's instructions on this issue and move forward with the understanding that if we choose to ignore our weight challenges, then we are choosing to sin with a deliberate spirit.

Let's choose obedience instead and move forward in faith. God can and will provide the strength we need to make a drastic change in the way we view food. Once we admit that we are feeding not just our bodies, but indulging our fleshly desires, we can begin to make a change.

He will provide the will, the desire, and the knowledge to create successful eating habits and to lose the weight we need to in order to restore our physical health and continue in our spiritual growth.

God calls each of us into His service in one form or another.

If anyone speaks, let him speak as the Oracles of God. If anyone ministers, let him do it as with the ability which God supplies, that in all things God may be glorified through Jesus Christ, to whom belong the glory and the dominion forever and ever. Amen.
I Peter 4:11

If you have been looking for a way to share God's message to those you love, your family, your co-workers or the world in general, let your weight loss and new-way-of-eating be your witness. A witness to God's glory, His strength, and His unending love. Show the world that you are a True Believer and that you are striving to encompass God's Word in its entirety in all aspects of your life. Follow the guidelines provided in this book, stay in prayer, and study your Bible daily. Ask God for the strength you need to accomplish those goals you set for yourself in both your physical and spiritual transformation. Then let your life speak for itself.

RESOURCES

WEBSITES AND MISCELLANEOUS SOURCES
https://www.ruled.me
https://ketogenic.com
https://dietdoctor.com
Https://ketosizeme.com
https://ketoresource.org
https://ketogenic-diet-rersource.com
https://myketokitchen.com

RECOMMENDED BOOKS

The Art and Science of Low Carb Living
by Jeff S. Volek, PhD, RD and Stephen D. Phinney, MD, PhD

Keto Clarity: Your Definitive Guide to the Benefits of a Low-Carb,
High-Fat Diet (2014)
 by Jimmy Moore with Eric C. Westman, MD

Low Carb, High Fat Food Revolution (2014)
by Dr Adreas Eenfeldt

Ketogenic Diet Mistakes: You Wish You Knew (2014)
By Sara Givens

MEDICAL JOURNALS: Recommended Reading
Comparison of the Atkins, Ornish, Weight Watchers, and Zone
diets for weight loss and heart disease risk reduction: a
randomized trial
https://jamanetwork.com/journals/jama/fullarticle/200094

ABOUT THE AUTHOR

 Barbara Hale is an Ordained Minister with the Universal Life Church. As a dedicated Christian women's counselor and nutritional researcher, she has a passion for helping people reach their goals of optimum health and spiritual maturity.

By offering training aids, study guides, and pamphlets designed to enlighten, encourage, and offer guidance to improving the quality of day-to-day living, Reverend Hale encourages women from all walks of life to learn to study the scriptures efficiently.

Made in the USA
Columbia, SC
24 July 2021